D1592318

Street Soccer: The Coaches' Guide

This book has been very carefully prepared, but no responsibility is taken for the correctness of the information it contains. Neither the author nor the publisher can assume liability for any damages or injuries resulting from information contained in this book.

DARREN LAVER

STREET SOCCER:
THE COACHES' GUIDE

COACHING PEOPLE CREATING PLAYERS

Meyer & Meyer Sport

EMMA S. CLARK MEMORIAL LIBRARY
Setauket, L.I., New York 11733

British Library Cataloguing in Publication Data
A catalogue record for this book is available from the British Library

Street Soccer: The Coaches' Guide
Maidenhead: Meyer & Meyer Sport (UK) Ltd., 2016
ISBN 978-1-78255-087-7

All rights reserved, especially the right to copy and distribute, including the translation rights. No part of this work may be reproduced — including by photocopy, microfilm or any other means — processed, stored electronically, copied or distributed in any form
whatsoever without the written permission of the publisher.

© 2016 by Meyer & Meyer Sport (UK) Ltd.
Aachen, Auckland, Beirut, Cairo, Cape Town, Dubai, Hägendorf, Hong Kong,
Indianapolis, Manila, New Delhi, Singapore, Sydney, Tehran, Vienna

  Member of the World Sport Publishers' Association (WSPA)

Manufacturing: Print Consult GmbH, München
E-Mail: info@m-m-sports.com
www.m-m-sports.com

TABLE OF CONTENTS

TABLE OF FIGURES

ACKNOWLEDGEMENT

I wish to personally thank the following people for their contributions to my inspiration and knowledge in creating this book. Thank you to every coach and player that has shaped my methods and making the coach I am today. Thank you to some very inspirational mentors Malcolm Cook, Simon Hartley, Matthew Gernaat and a big thank you to Gareth Long who continues to work alongside me in developing the creative game of soccer.

ABOUT THE AUTHOR

Darren Laver is one of the most unique and creative coaches in the world. He is the founder of the International Street Soccer Association (ISSA) and the street soccer concept, and is a globally recognized expert coach and exhibition performer.

Street soccer was born out of Mr. Laver's growing disappointment with the traditional coaching and teaching methods so widespread throughout the United Kingdom. Based on his creativity in teaching street soccer and the distinguished organization he created in 2006, he is widely respected as an expert. It was self-evident that the gulf between soccer mechanical skills and creativity was growing, and Mr. Laver has revolutionized the coaching process to remedy these gaps.

He is a recognized authority on the subject, and his performances and exhibitions have allowed coaches, teachers and those involved in the biggest sport in the world to seek more creative, efficient and dynamic ways to coach this beautiful game. Mr. Laver has brought together some of the most influential, creative concepts in the game from all over the world to develop skillful players.

Using the International Street Soccer Association (ISSA) as a platform, Mr. Laver has dedicated his life to coaching players to improve their creative skill. He provides training programs and street soccer events for amateur, youth and professional clubs, councils and communities with the ISSA training license across the world. Mr. Laver's influence has grown to be a worldwide phenomenon, with global titan Thomas Cook running ISSA programs in many of their holiday resorts across Europe, featuring Mr. Laver as a performer. Mr. Laver is also the founder of the famous Creative Skill Camps that runs across North America and Canada, using street soccer as a means to develop skillful players.

Mr. Laver has lent his expertise and performances to the Union of European Football Associations (UEFA), providing skill-training tutorials with Danish international soccer player, Brian Laudrup, for whom he was selected to run a series of events and exhibitions across Denmark. For SoccerEx in Africa, Mr. Laver exhibited his skills, and in the UK engaged with young adults for the BBC *Your Game* tour.

Mr. Laver is recognized as one of the leading street soccer coaches and soccer skill performers in the world. He has also been recognized for his extraordinary coaching skills and performance abilities in a variety of published books including *Street Football* published by Wayland Publishers in 2013, and has published numerous articles on the importance of creative thinking including an article for the NSCAA Coaching Journal in 2015. In 2011, Mr. Laver's extraordinary abilities and performances led him to being voted one of the best street soccer players in the United Kingdom, and he was the selected to be one of 45 star players to feature in EA Sports FIFA Street (2012 video game).

FOREWORD ON STREET SOCCER

Apart from those blessed with a natural talent, the vast majority of players require some level of training or coaching before they can compete at the highest levels of the discipline. This is where rules are established and we begin to play according to set patterns. The experts tell us that this is the only way to ensure consistency. Amateurs can afford to make plenty of mistakes because they really have nothing to lose but their pride. However, even that is only temporary. At the professional level things change significantly. Here we are expected to win and win again. We either establish a pattern of dominance or are consigned to that undesirable space between losing streaks and embarrassing mediocrity.

Modern technology and techniques have created plenty of opportunities for learning but they also demand a lot from us. One of the complaints from players is that modern coaches have simply lost the will to have fun. They focus so much on details and goals that they forget that they are working with a human being who can get bored. Soccer players in particular thrive in creative and exciting environments that give their talents the space to shine brightly. This does not mean that we forget the basic concepts and techniques; rather, it requires that we coach with a bit of imagination and excitement. This book attempts to change the mindset by revolutionizing the following process of typical coaching practice:

1. Introducing successful core techniques which lead to player development
2. Crafting a thinking game once progress has been achieved
3. Encouraging teamwork and support from large and small groups
4. Implementing what has been learnt by way of small-sided games

The typical way of coaching is full of content but also suffers from some level of tediousness and is likely to inspire boredom in the player due to its long-windedness. In fact the drills that are demonstrated time and time again can begin to take away from the art of playing soccer. It then ceases to be the beautiful game and instead turns into yet another repetitive activity. We suggest that the only way to make coaching work is to make it practical. Doing instead of just thinking is one of the great interest points for natural soccer players. We want to tap into that. That is what modern coaching science is all about. We attempt to overcome the shortcomings of traditional coaching systems. This book is presented after extensive research, anecdotal evidence and the practical experience of actually coaching soccer players. It is indeed all about the exciting phenomenon that is street soccer.

INTRODUCTION

"Street Soccer is for everyone who refuses to let their individuality, creativity and imagination die."[1]

This book has been written for all those interested in making coaching a success for soccer. It is aimed not only at the coaches but also the players who are being prepared for great things. It is relevant to the coach, parents and soccer clubs who want talent to come up and be nurtured. We have tried to present complex theories and methods in a language that is accessible to people who engage in soccer on a day-to-day basis. Therefore we hope that this book will outline the basic principles that are critical for the successful implementation of a street soccer coaching program. We believe that our approach is special because it is different from anything you may have encountered so far. The coaching style that we adopt can completely revolutionize the way in which we handle players, particularly in the delicate stages of their development when they are not completely in tune with the sport.

We are often inundated with questions from readers and we suspect this is because our one-of-a-kind training programs pique everyone's interest. Nevertheless we believe that this book provides you with a firm foundation for understanding what we are trying to do and how it can help you. All our exercises and sessions are very modern in their approach

1   *The International Street Soccer Association, 2015*

but they are firmly grounded in the best knowledge about soccer. We do not believe in following the mainstream just for the sake of conforming. That is why this book thinks outside the box and encourages you to do so in return.

The beauty of street soccer is the fact that it challenges a lot of things you may have heard about coaching. We do not lightly abandon the models that have been used before us for years. There is a very good reason why we are prepared to explore this new radical approach. For example, we are not convinced that the traditional approach to tactics is really the best way to prepare players for the ever-changing game. This book casts a critical eye on how coaches train aspiring soccer players. We use all the knowledge that we have about human learning in order to suggest radical but effective ways of achieving great results. This book is written from the standpoint of actual evidence and knowledge of working with players. It is not just about theory but the things that have been proven time and time again.

By reading this book and implementing some of the things we recommend, you can begin to create an optimal learning environment for the budding soccer player. They will be able to pick up a lot of skills and have lots of fun in the process. Street soccer is all about vibrancy and creativity. The chapters will take you through the process of heating things up and intriguing the interest of your learners every single day. We believe the originality and the courage to stand by your principles is one of the reasons for success in sport. Therefore this book is anything but a copy of previous styles. It is new and it is challenging. It is the future of a brand of soccer that will have everyone sitting up and paying attention.

This book is also quite detailed in terms of giving you all the tools that you need when you are running a street soccer session. We emphasize practicality over complexity. This book tells you the what, why, how and where of modern soccer coaching, and includes 25 fun street soccer games, produced for developing thinking players. We have given a lot of thought to making them as relevant to you as possible. They are high impact and inspirational activities that will leave your players wanting more and more of your time with them. We hope you enjoy reading this book. We certainly have enjoyed writing it for you. Let us begin by looking at what makes a great player.

CHAPTER 1

UNDERSTANDING GREAT PLAYERS

"The difference between a successful person and others is not a lack of strength, not a lack of knowledge, but rather a lack of will." Vince Lombardi (1913-1970) [2]

If you look at soccer today, the really elite players are few and far in between. It is this scarcity of exceptionalism that allows the top class to reap unbelievable benefits. Some (like Cristiano Ronaldo, Lionel Messi, Zinedine Zidane, Diego Maradona, Marta Vieira da Silva, Pelé Edson Arantes do Nascimento and Johan Cruyff) have become household names thus transcending the arenas that gave them so much glory. Their accomplishments are unquestionable and they include such glorious exploits like multiple World Cup victories and countless international trophies. However, it is not only the personalities that appeal but also their approach to the game. We admire them because they bring something different to the pitch and therefore entertain millions of people across the globe. Some of their technical abilities have acquired mythical status but each has one thing in common with the other: they are creative. Their coaching and training did not stifle this innate ability; on the contrary, many of them became even more creative as they matured.

---

2   *NFL Football Coach (Green Bay Packers)*

There are many ingredients that go into the pot that is player development in soccer (see Figure 1). The influences are varied and their impact can be negative or positive. Some players thrive on adversity and are able to come out kicking on the other side even if the beginning was rather uncomfortable. Others are blessed with incredible talent which allows them to do things that we thought impossible before we saw them. There is yet another group that has limited talent but more than makes up for this hindrance through extraordinary hard work. They will go back to the same drill until they have it perfect. There is no one single element that is the magical key to success; people have different talents and capabilities that they call upon when they are required to deliver victory. The stories of these great players are so inspirational that some ambitious young players attempt to copy all the things that have happened. You are not going to recreate a Ronaldo any time soon. It is far better to create your own brand of greatness.

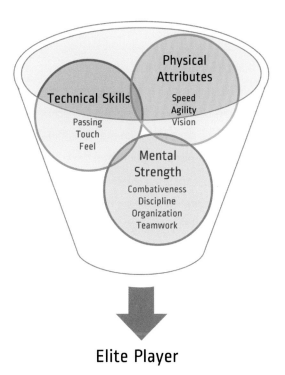

Figure 1: The Attributes of a Great Soccer Player

THE UNIQUENESS OF SOCCER

Soccer is a game of opportunities and there are many paths to the same destination. That is why we enjoy watching different teams during the World Cup. You can admire the work ethic and tactical discipline of the Germans while also enjoying the flare of the Brazilians or the passion of the Italians. At one point or another each of these national teams have been able to win. If all they presented was one brand then the spectators would soon get bored with soccer. Within each of these teams, there will be a number of great players who are often called the talisman or leader. When they are on the pitch things seem to go marvelously well. When they are off then the team begins to crumble. These great players have their own brand of magic which makes them indispensable to the sport and the teams that they work with.

If there is one thing that my experience within the higher echelons of soccer has taught me, it is the fact that the possibilities are infinite. These great players provide us with insight that is bigger than anything we have ever seen. They cease to be learners and become teachers on the pitch because they get things right in an effortless swing. At the same time, these great players occasionally come up with a trick that makes a potentially dull match very memorable even for those who are not intimately acquainted with the sport. Sometimes the great talent does not appear on the scene immediately. It may take time, but at one point or the other, the great soccer player is going to show what they are really about. By looking at the journeys of these great players, we can also improve our own development as coaches and even as active participants in soccer. These players are role models. Even those that face spectacular falls can become inspirational because we learn not to make the mistakes that they have made before.

WHAT MAKES THE STARS EXTRAORDINARY?

Working with some of these elite athletes has taught me that appearances can be deceiving and that a background does not always foretell the feature. It is always an honor to work with world class players but what is even more humbling is the fact that many of them have overcome substantial odds in order to be where they are today. Another startling fact is that despite their great achievements, these world-class players remain human just like you and me. They hurt, they feel pain, they laugh, they triumph, they are moody, they have doubts, they get frustrated and they do all those things that make us humans. Yet these players retain an exceptional gift that becomes instantly recognizable the moment they start playing. It is through nurturing and planned development over a long period of time that their skills have been harnessed to the extent that they can overcome some of their human weaknesses.

There are a few things that make a player really stand out. One of them is perception. Their cognitive wiring is such that they are able to pick up the most complex of moves and store them in their brain to be retrieved in the heat of a match. Moreover these great players are also blessed with exceptional hand-eye coordination. Their bodies are in harmony and they can will the muscles to do what is required. That does not take away from their humanity. Rather it emphasizes the great lengths to which they have gone to deliver such qualities despite their human weaknesses. These people master so many skills and are more than happy to practice until they get it perfect. Although their bodies may be aching, their higher calling to sports excellence means that they continue to practice in order to achieve the perfection that they desire. It is not good enough to have a decent pass, volley or touch; you have to develop a level of athleticism that is really quite extraordinary in order to compete at the highest levels of the sport.

Another important element is that of mental strength. A great player knows that they are great and wants to show the competition what they can do. They have such self-belief that even when the match appears to be slipping away, they will continue trying until they pull out the win. Great players are very consistent and are able to go on a seemingly endless winning streak. In all this, it becomes clear that talent alone is not a passport to greatness. You need to invest in player development and also work hard in order to turn that talent into numerous diverse soccer skills. Coaches tend to identify where the weaknesses are and then take systematic steps in order to ensure that those weaknesses are either completely eliminated or mitigated by the development of other key strengths. For example, a player with poor touch can be taught to move better and get into positions where they may score goals without necessarily having to use excellent touch.

The top athletes are not satisfied with what they have at the moment. That is why they continuously seek opportunities to take their talents to the next level. A coach is absolutely essential, particularly in the earlier stages when the player may not necessarily have all the background knowledge that is required to make it into world-class soccer. An oft-repeated mantra is "Hard work beats talent every time if talent does not work hard." All things being equal, the player who puts in the most effort is likely to get the most rewards from the game. Early and consistent preparation is therefore the key to being match-ready. There are so many tests, challenges and obstacles in soccer, the least of which is the existence of very strong teams with changing tactics. Those that rely on talent alone are never going to make it.

WHAT DOES REAL SUCCESS ENTAIL IN SPORT?

The first thing that drives top athletes is passion. Vallerand et al. (2007) found that the development of expertise (and therefore improved performance) is linked to the passion the participant has for the activity they are engaged in. They exist for the sport and their love of it is unconditional. They do not mind bad weather, grumpy teammates or even hostile fans. What they want to do is go out there and perform. These are the people that understand the craft and science behind soccer. They have chased this dream for years and are therefore not prepared to give up until the body can no longer support their endeavors. It is also important to remember that the shelf-life of a soccer player is not infinite. By the time they hit their late thirties, their best days are gone. Therefore it is important for them to make the most of the time that they have at their peak. Figure 2 shows that training, a sound technical base and supportive parents are the three most important drivers of elite player development.

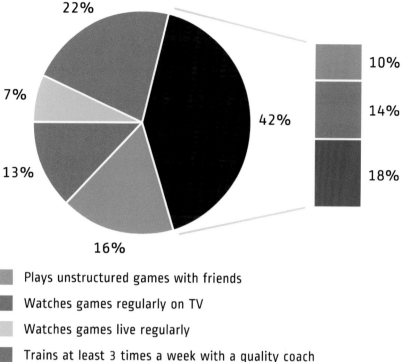

Plays unstructured games with friends

Watches games regularly on TV

Watches games live regularly

Trains at least 3 times a week with a quality coach

Supportive Parents

Highly competitive by nature

Source: (Young, 2012)

Figure 2: Elite Player Ingredients

The passion that great players have is the main reason that they are able to dedicate a significant proportion of their waking lives to the sport. In the more advanced cases, the player is so self-motivated that it almost as if the services of their coach as superfluous. Colvin (2008) argues that because practice is tedious; players require a spark that makes them want to do it. Thus greatness requires a certain amount of dedication even where the enjoyment is not always constantly present. The occasional frustrations that the players face are yet another test of their resolve and commitment.

TAPPING INTO THE PLAYFUL SPIRIT

Playing without passion will soon tire even the most enthusiastic soccer player. The amount of commitment required for greatness is such that only someone with a real love of the game will be able to carry on, particularly in the face of adversity. Some might say that this is really all about character but coaches can help to build character, strengthening it and making it formidable. Soccer at the highest levels requires an abundance of energy which is born out of things that are beyond physical power or even adrenaline. It is more of a spirit that is unbreakable. The glamour and financial rewards only come later on.

These ideas are not merely anecdotal. They are rooted in serious psychological research and proven theories. For example they are in line with the self-determination theory (Ryan & Deci, 2000) and harmonious passion (Vallerand R. J., 2008). Vallerand in particular argues that people will voluntarily choose to engage in those activities that ignite their passions. Therefore some of the motivation is already established and is intrinsic to them. Although coaches can create motivation or coax it out of their students, it is the intrinsic variety that is more durable, stable and powerful.

Once the motivation is established then the great players move on to building their resilience and perseverance. Players develop such a strong will that they are able to withstand incredible levels of discomfort on the pitch and off it in the pursuit of their goals; this is why world class athletes are able to train for long periods even if they are winning a lot. They have this hunger to do better and achieve more which to some seems inexplicable. One of the most remarkable phenomena is when an athlete is able to invest so much in order to acquire a tiny competitive advantage that can make the difference in a tight match. It is a classic case of full commitment and unwavering determination.

WHAT IS THE METHODOLOGY OF LEARNING TO WIN?

It is through this passion that players can acquire a level of inquisitiveness about the game which almost borders on obsession. They are relentless in their quest to know more and can tire out a poorly prepared coach. More importantly, they do not ignore the details and subtlety so easy to overlook when focusing on the bigger picture of winning. Quite often this unique part of the journey will start when the elite athlete begins to separate themselves from the pack. They put in more hours and develop an even closer relationship with their coach because they want to gain that extra bit. It is during this process that they achieve the maturity that will see them through the turbulence of playing.

From the outset, the great player will recognize their weaknesses and will immediately start developing protective strategies which are designed to compensate for those less-than-glorious aspects of their game. Their desire for perfection seems too intense but that is what is required at this level. Great coaches thrive on this intensity and improve their own practices in order to keep up with the pace. Here the elite athlete will begin to take calculated risks. They will play around with their soccer ball until they find the right balance. It becomes a case of increasing possibilities and making daring moves. At the same time the great player is not a clown on the pitch who entertains but fails to win the game. Instead they overcome every obstacle in their way with focus, knowing that failure is not an option.

Deep passion ignites the curiosity which in turn brings out all the core characteristics of greatness in these players. The preeminent psychologist Loewenstein (1994) argued that curiosity is a form of passion because it tends to carry a significant amount of motivational intensity which can be translated into enthusiasm for any given activity such as learning. He suggests that we use these forces in order to understand and survive our environment, an idea that can be applied to a soccer field dotted with opposing colleagues and teammates.

CAN TALENT ALONE TAKE YOU TO THE TOP?

It is undeniable that there are people who are born with something special. They have a talent which is a gift from nature, thus making things slightly easier for them in a given sport. The critical thing is whether these talents are nurtured and developed over a long time or left to fester until they are virtually obsolete. Some people are unable to nurture their talents due to circumstances beyond their control such as injury or lack of financial support. Others simply lack the drive to explore the possibilities and settle for amateurism or even mediocrity. This serves to demonstrate that an excellent athlete in any field must be able to combine their natural talent with passion in order to achieve this heightened state of achievement. Coaching should be introduced as soon as practicable. In the next chapter we consider the learning process and apply that knowledge to the conceptualization of street soccer.

SUMMARY

- Great players can be born or made. Hard work and the right techniques will often surpass unapplied talent. The acquisition of technical skills is a long process that requires expert handling and patience.

- Physical discipline must be accompanied by psychological endurance in order to create consistency. Players must develop the habit of winning. This is the indomitable spirit that separates the also-rans from the truly big stage movers of soccer.

- The elite players start early, while the cognitive and physical dimensions of their true capability can be shaped. The coach is there to discover, encourage and provide new avenues for development.

🔸 The psychology of a player is often as important as their physical elements. Players must be in a good place mentally in order to perform well on the pitch. It is important to acknowledge that great sports people remain human beings. They have the same hopes and fears like everybody else. Therefore support from a good coach is of the essence.

🔸 Role models in sport are not just about what achievements that people have made but also the way in which they came to those achievements. It is important to look at the journey as well as the outcome for the player.

STREET SOCCER AND THE LEARNING PROCESS

"Soccer is an art not a science and the game should be played attractively as well as effectively. Soccer is a game of skill, imagination, creativity and decision-making. Coaching should not stifle, but enhance those elements."
Bobby Howe[3]

There is an unfortunate misconception that the sole purpose of coaching is to create players that are technically able to win more games. It is this eye-on-the-prize mentality that obscures some of the best traditions of coaching. Although winning is desirable and a great validation of all the work that the coach has invested in the student, it is nothing more than one of the many byproducts of good coaching. It is true that coaches look to improve the techniques and tactical awareness of their prodigies but they also want to create better people in the broadest sense. The physical capabilities are then accompanied by a maturity of interpersonal skills, social interaction and psychological fortitude.

---

3   *(US Soccer: Former Director of Coaching, Professional and National Team Coach)*

At the same time it is important to acknowledge that coaches are responsible for guiding and educating those that are under their charge. This implies that a diligent coach must always try to update their skills and teaching methods in order to reach the highest industry standards. Ultimately it is not just about expediency but also the effectiveness of the coaching method that has been selected for that particular athlete.

AN ENGLISH SOCCER CASE STUDY

The English Football Association (FA) provides us with some salutary lessons. Although the FA was founded way back in 1863 to govern the soccer industry in England, it was not until the English side failed to qualify for the UEFA cup in 2008 that someone decided that it was time to develop a coaching strategy guide for this auspicious association. During that transformative process, it was openly acknowledged that there was no English style to speak of. Yes, the players had technical and tactical advantages but they woefully lacked individuality (creativity, elegance, bravado, etc.) to pair with their much-vaunted skills. The result of these deficiencies were unexpectedly mediocre performances on the big stage.

The problems were being manifested by way of the hapless responses to one-on-one pressure situations. The players did not understand tempo and could not maintain momentum for long periods of time. They seemed prisoners of a rehearsed brand of soccer that was unable to respond to the unexpected. Meanwhile the fans were baying for blood when the English side was continuously exposed by their European opponents who were able to display an amazing versatility well beyond the meager capabilities of the home talents. Hiring and sacking national soccer team managers on a seasonal basis was not having the positive impact that had been hoped for. Clearly there was a need to review the entire coaching strategy of the organization.

In their response to these problems, the FA showed an exemplary ability to engage in a process of self-criticism. The new coaching guide acknowledged the need to modernize the approaches that had been used for years. One area of particular interest was the continual development mechanism (CPD), which involves developing the physical and technical qualities of the players while simultaneously addressing their psychosocial needs. The fact that it took the FA so long to reach this point is a testament to the fact that even the most prestigious institutions are prone to obvious mistakes when they do not regularly engage in self-examination. Nevertheless their recognition of the need to make fundamental improvements is admirable. Under the new framework, the FA intends to produce world-class players who are not afraid of the big arenas. On the other hand, there is still something missing. We do not yet see how these lofty goals are going to be achieved. What they really need are clear philosophies and proven educative structures. Perhaps our view of coaching inside out might give the FA some ideas.

INSIDE-OUT COACHING TECHNIQUES

Soccer coaching is not an isolated discipline. The fact that coaches are professionals means that they acquire knowledge from different disciplines and then apply it to the objectives that they want to achieve. This is the best way of optimizing and modernizing the entire learning process in sport. Individuals learn on both the micro and macro spheres. Therefore it becomes important to understand the intricacies of all these modalities so that the trained player can be comfortable in any one of them. Once we understand how the learning process actually works, we will be in a position to create the most conducive environments for this type of knowledge-skill acquisition to take place. The larger body of educational discipline has a lot to contribute toward soccer coaching which is indeed recognized as a pedagogic activity.

The fundamentals help in building the right aptitude. Therefore it becomes imperative to develop a clear outline of how players are able to develop their skills and use the intuition that is so critical to the game. We only have to look at our own learning processes in order to find the answers for the coaches. The brain is at the center of these processes because it is the one that makes decisions; it sends the requisite neurological messages to the muscles that move the body in a particular direction. The difference between elite athletes and everyone else is the fact that this transmission process is much faster and instinctive. A case in point is the much desired hand-eye coordination. Kicking a ball might seem easy but the complexity of the muscles involved can challenge the most advanced computer system today. Moreover the player has to be discerning in terms of the information that they process because they operate in a data-rich environment. There are appeals to all five senses, and if someone is distracted they will not be able to pick up the clues that the match is giving.

UNDERSTANDING THE WORKINGS OF THE HUMAN BRAIN

Different parts of the brain control different functions and all are essential for the survival of a human being. In coaching we try to enhance the efficacy of these functions in order to achieve difficult feats on the pitch. For example in lateralization (see Figure 3), the left hemisphere of the brain is more analytical, focusing on things such as cognition, processing and general thinking. The right hemisphere by contrast controls the non-thinking actions of the person particularly in the subconscious. Although the brain is a marvel of coordination, it sometimes struggles to process multiple strands of information at the same time. This is where good training comes in because the player is acclimatized to this type of multi-tasking until it becomes instinctive. In the end the player is able to make quick decisions just in time without having to spend time reorganizing all the different parts of their brain. Decisiveness is a very critical skill that a soccer player cannot do without in the professional sphere.

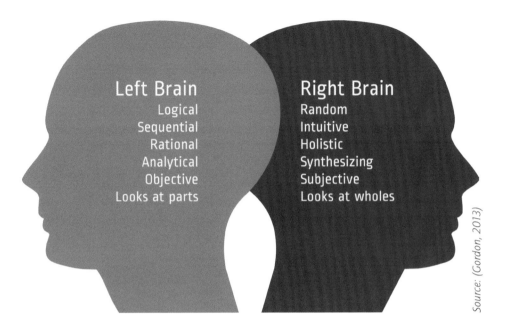

Source: (Gordon, 2013)

Figure 3: Left-Right Hemispherical Brain Lateralization in Functionality

As a coach or someone interested in the learning process, you will probably have heard about the triune model. It is very similar in approach to the lateralization of the brain above. However, the critical difference is that the triune model examines the brain from the inside out rather than from the outside in. It all begins with primitive art which then transforms into a lizard brain. Eventually we developed a mammalian brain which is the precursor to the human brain. The latter stage is distinguished by the development of a frontal cortex or neocortex. Figure 4 demonstrates the evolution of competencies until the triune model.

Lizard Brain	Mammal Brain	Human Brain
Brain stem & cerebelum	Limbic system	Neocortex
Fight or flight	Emotions, memories, haibits	Language, abstract thought, imagination, consciousness
Autopilot	Decisions	Reasons, rationalizes

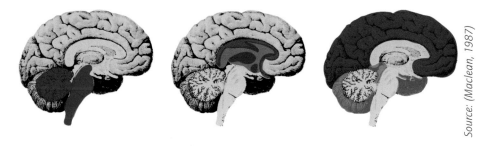

Source: (Maclean, 1987)

Figure 4: The Triune Brain Theory

According to Marshall (2014, p. 37) "the brain develops from the bottom up and inside to outside." The most primitive part of our brain is the lizard element. When it is in control the rest shuts down. At this stage we are programmed to either fight or escape from a perceived threat. It really is a survival instinct that served to protect our earliest ancestors when they were being hunted or faced with something new. The decision has to be made within a split second so there is no time for deep pondering of any sort. The problem is that this neocortex takes up a significant proportion of brain matter when compared to the other parts.

The younger players are sometimes confused about using this part of the brain. They end up trying to overanalyze things in a misguided attempt to impress their coach. The primitive brain is very instinctive and does not require too much thought. It is similar to a situation where players attempt to break down a skill into minute constituent parts but lose the overall objective of the skill in the process. A case in point is bending the ball. Although this move involves many processes, the elite players are able to perform it in one smooth motion and are not able to quite describe what they have done. Here the brain clears all the complex strategies and simply performs the required physical act.

This information is an important resource for coaches who are then able to use it in order to make their players perform better. It is relatively rare for people to encounter situations of mortal danger where they only have to use their reptilian brain. Therefore this aspect of their capabilities is applied elsewhere. In sport it is used to make quick instinctive decisions during critical moments of a match. It is also important to note the fact that the reptilian brain also has a darker side in as far as it has been associated with fear and shame. These are negative attributes for the soccer player because they tend to reduce their overall confidence. On the other hand younger children who are fearful or diffident may shut down the more complex parts of their brain, instead focusing on the reptilian response of fight or flight. Soccer requires a lot more sophistication than that so it is important to develop other parts of the brain and use them when appropriate. Marshall (2014) suggests that "The trick is to help them to calm down and feel safe so that the reptilian part of the brain becomes inactive and the frontal cortex can then become active."

SAFE LEARNING ZONES

This kind of environment has become a common feature of coaching and mentoring in sport. A safe zone does wonders for the confidence of the player both on and off the pitch. Once a player is self-confident, they can use their brain resources to focus without any distractions. They need not second-guess their actions because they know that they are doing the right thing. This assurance is sometimes unconscious in its presentation and is certainly done without any hint of self-consciousness. Players can then achieve a fluid state in which the brain function is in tandem with their objectives. The concerns about fight or flight are relegated to secondary importance.

Such a paradigm suggests that it is far more profitable for the resourceful coach to focus on both the left and right brains. The left will set the logical patterns of thinking while the right will ensure that the instinctive parts of the game are dealt with effectively. Unfortunately some of the modern coaching has been reduced to nothing more than a logical and sequential delivery of question-and-answer formats, designed to accelerate the acquisition of knowledge about soccer skills rather than the soccer skills themselves. Such an approach is more suited to simple mathematics rather than the beautiful game. A player has to actually have the skills; it is less important for them to be able to write eloquently about those skills.

The inside-out approach ensures that the player is emotionally and psychologically in the right place so that they can execute the physical skills that are part and parcel of soccer. The right brain is responsible for ensuring that the player has learned the skill even before they have fully experienced it. Human beings are normally born with more than 10 billon cells about half of which are not necessary for later life. Thus once it enters adolescence, the brain begins to systematically shave off those neurons that are superfluous. According to Marshall (2014), "if a cell is not used regularly for any reason, its connection will just fall away." Coaches therefore must ensure that the brain is used fully rather than letting it go to waste. Process or bureaucracy is very important when trying to achieve this process.

BREAKING THE BONDS OF EDUCATIONAL BUREAUCRACY

Traditionally there has been a kind of cross-purpose meeting point between the implementation of soccer coaching and the workings of the human beings. It is only once a bridge is successfully constructed between these two disciplines that we can consistently produce players that are worthy of a world-class status. The first thing to acknowledge is that, more often than not, the brain wants success. This is the same thing that the coach desires. So we can say that from the outset there is an element of commonality. This can be the foundation of much closer collaboration. The player's brain becomes an ally and tool for the coach. Similarly the knowledge and experience of the coach takes the brain through a kind of gym or remedial program so that it can perform much better practically. The successful teams are the ones that have achieved this symbiosis.

STREET SOCCER

Some of this dysfunction is down to the misguided modern educational structure. For some inexplicable reason, the education system tends to ignore the right brain and the aptitudes that it can bring to learners. Thus the people who graduate from these schools are very good at memorization, logic, analysis and passing standardized tests, but they are less good at harnessing their instincts and creative thinking. We suggest that the brain works better when both sides are working in tandem rather than if one of them is isolated.

Any physical skills like driving or riding a bike requires both sides of the brain to work in tandem. You need some proprioceptive aptitudes in addition to the muscle capabilities in order to accomplish the said task. Because we are in tune with both sides of our brain, the task seems simple, even trivial, when in reality there are so many complex processes that are involved. Take, for example, swimming; when you think too much about floating, you drown but once you have acquired that skill, everything comes naturally. You are relaxed and the water responds by giving you buoyancy. Indeed once the neural connections are made and strengthened, they often last well into our old age. That is why it is possible for a pianist to play a complex piece of music even after years of being out of practice.

Complaints about our current education system notwithstanding, it is useful to consider their origins and objectives. Mitra (2013) argues that the predominant pedagogic dogma today is a relic of the colonial empires, particularly of Britain, resulting in the need for an obedient bureaucratic administrative machine that brooks no creativity or independent thought. In the colonial empires, all that was required of learners was to write legibly so that they could maintain administrative records; to read to a basic level sufficient for understanding the instructions given to them in writing; and to do simple mental mathematics. Occasionally the privileged were allowed one other skill (such as playing the guitar) in order to break the tedium of this static learning process. The students that graduated from these colonial and post-colonial institutions were mere functionaries and not independent thinkers by any stretch of the imagination. Those that sought to change the order in anything perceived to be a radical way were quickly eliminated from the highest ranks of the bureaucracy.

Sadly a lot of sports coaching practice has failed to completely break away from this damaging mold. Players are taught to simply execute the plan that the coach has in mind. Their creativity is restrained in favor of easy success. However, there is no guarantee that the people these players meet on the soccer field are going to play according to the script. They may come up with all sorts of imaginative things that can throw the campaign off. That is why it is imperative to develop learning environments that can foster the individuality, creativity, flair and enthusiasm of the players that we coach.

SUMMARY

- Human beings like play. They enjoy innovating and would prefer the opportunity to showcase their creativity. Great coaching not only piques the curiosity of players but also increases their motivation to learn more. This is a recognition of the innate human artist that Picasso talked about[4].

- Originality and flair in a soccer player is a function of their passion and talent. It reflects the fact that their learning has been enjoyable and memorable. Coaches encourage a mindset of creativity by providing a stimulating environment and developing supportive relationships with their wards.

- Creativity in play is the way to solve the unexpected problems that soccer players find on the pitch. It prepares them for difficulties, challenges and obstacles in a way that makes their success durable. In doing so they are required to use both their analytical and physical talents to the maximum.

---

4   *"Every child is an artist. The problem is how to remain an artist once he grows up." Pablo Picasso as quoted in Peter (1979, p. 25).*

- There are three critical aspects of the whole-brain learning paradigm. They include the ability to immerse oneself into any given activity with total commitment; the ability to achieve a state of relaxed alertness even during periods of stress; and a knack for simulating scenarios in order to actively process available information.

- The labor-intensive 10,000-hour rule of sports training is a flawed theory because of its false assumption of quantitative notions. Not every hour of training will create a commensurate measure of skill acquisition. Therefore the qualitative aspects of training must also be addressed.

- Creativity as a concept has three critical components that are aligned in a flow states paradigm. These include challenges that fully test our capabilities; interesting scenarios that tickle our curiosity; and the confidence to tackle those difficulties based on our capabilities.

In order to merge the current coaching-educational practice with the best aspects of play, it is imperative to have the right conducive environment. The next chapter tackles this process in detail.

OPTIMIZING THE LEARNING ENVIRONMENT

"Bring out their strengths to allow them to be successful. Modify their assignments to meet their individual needs. To encourage creativity, allow children to make choices about what they learn..."[5]

In order to create a conducive learning environment, coaches must identify a place which they imbue with the best equipment available and then set the stage for productive knowledge-skill acquisition. In addition there are intangibles that should not be forgotten including confidence, motivation and creativity or play. The principles are only useful to the coach if they can be applied to a real-life situation. Without motivation, learners will not be able to ask the why of their sport. It is the glue that makes decision making coherent in as far as the learner is trying to justify the opportunity cost of engaging in the learning activity. For many players, the decision to opt for soccer is conscious and based on factual issues.

Motivated players are able to train for long periods even when their bodies are injured or tired. It is not enough to simply state that motivation is the answer because there are many things that go into the mix. Remember that motivation can be negative or positive. For example some coaches attempt to re-live past glories through their wards. It takes

---

5   (Davis, 2004, p. 39)

time and effort for this motivation to translate into results. Lionel Messi once commented that took him "17 years and 114 days to become an overnight success"[6]. In the same vein, it is not advisable for the motivations to be imposed from the outside. Parents, coaches and sponsors must have the patience and presence of mind to allow the players to develop their own motivations without external interference.

DURABLE MOTIVATIONS AND RESULTS

Extrinsic motivation has a role in sports particularly if the player does not seem to be taking the initiative. However, such extrinsic motivation can only take them so far. If there is a crisis, then it is likely that the player without intrinsic motivation is going to give up regardless of whether the other people around them are cheering them on. By the same token, the lack of a supportive external environment can create cognitive difficulties for the player to the extent that their intrinsic motivation is challenged to the furthest borders of its limits. That is why it is so important for coaches to fully embrace their supportive roles. That means understanding some of the different motivators for human beings as demonstrated in Figure 5.

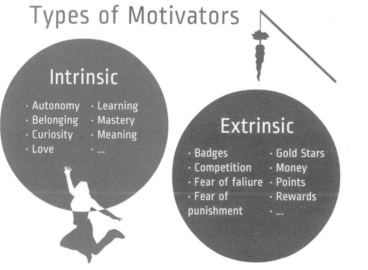

Figure 5: Intrinsic and Extrinsic Motivation

6   *(All LYBIO, 1987)*

STREET SOCCER

Street soccer is about getting people to enjoy soccer first and foremost. That is when they gain the curiosity that drives them to continue with the sport even when conditions are not ideal. We give you the tips to increase the level of engagement and ultimately the fun that the learner has while acquiring skills and capabilities that could possibly turn them into a real star on the global stage. At the same time we are not interested in churning out identical players with identical problems. We would rather see people embrace their difference and individuality, and turn them into competitive advantages.

Confidence necessarily emanates from a feeling of success. It is also one of the reasons why confident people are paradoxically more motivated than those who are not. Because they have seen the rewards of sport and know that they have what it takes to access those rewards, the confident players keep going even when the rest of the world is telling them to give up. To that end, the learning environment must provide interest as well as challenges.

JUDGEMENT-FREE LEARNING ENVIRONMENTS

All our lives we are judged on a range of things including how we look, how we speak, where we were born and even our personality. The same can be said of sports. A coach that continuously negatively judges learners is going to dampen their enthusiasm. This kind of downcast approach can become a self-fulfilling prophecy where the player begins to believe that there is no realistic possibility of them succeeding, thus giving up on what could potentially have been their dream profession. By contrast, a judgment-free learning environment fosters the right confidence in the learner (see Figure 6). They self-justify their involvement soccer by the fact that their coach believes in them.

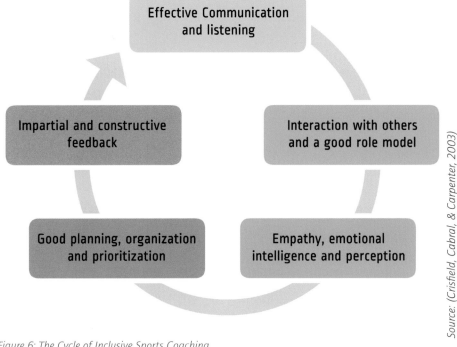

Source: (Crisfield, Cabral, & Carpenter, 2003)

Figure 6: The Cycle of Inclusive Sports Coaching

The highest level of sport requires an ability to experiment and recover from failure. A learning environment that continuously focuses on the negative will eventually lead to cautiousness and timidity. That translates into unwillingness to take risks both on and off the pitch. The fear of failure can be a real debilitating experience for a soccer player particularly in the early development stage. The people who have been poorly coached are the ones that will never play offensively because they fear losing more than they desire to win.

Using a positive approach, the coach allows the player to fully embrace and utilize their problem-solving skills. Some solutions may not work immediately but at least there is a clear indicator that the player knows the process of experimentation and is willing to do it without prompting. Nothing is more impressive on the pitch than a player that is creative. They bring so much joy not only to their teammates but also the spectators who find something that is very different from what they are used to. The beauty of using a person-centered coaching style is that it accounts for the quirks that make us human. You learn to tap into the unique qualities of that player that you wish to turn into a star. Although there are basic standards of performance; they are never rigid and can be adjusted accordingly[7].

The diversity of human nature is the key to the ethos that we follow in street soccer. Each one of us is born with a physiological and neurological makeup, a good proportion of which is made in the womb. Fetuses already have neurological networks as they bounce about in the amniotic fluid. This is the beginning of movement in response to the environment, a capability that can make all the difference later in life if one decides to become an athlete. As the child grows, the differences are emphasized since people develop at varying rates. It is therefore imperative for the coach to really know their athlete before designing a training program.

---

7   *"No one knows the right answer, no one knows precisely what will happen...no one can produce the desired future, on demand. Some people are better at guessing than others, but not by much.... In fact, the gap isn't between the people who know and those that don't. It's between the people who show up with their best work, and those that hold back..." Seth Godin (Author and Entrepreneur) from Ramsden (2015)*

PLAYING FOR SUCCESS

Street soccer uses play, one of the most effective pedagogic tools, to achieve the experimentation that is critical to modern soccer. This is the avenue through which youngsters and not-so-youngsters can be introduced to experimentation. We have much to learn from animals which for centuries have been teaching their young life skills using play. Even the hunter and killer instinct has some of those competitive overtones which are critical to winning soccer matches. Since we are all slaves to evolution, genuine learning can best be achieved by looking back at what our ancestors did. Of course we refine their ways for modern audiences but the principles remain the same.

So what is play? It has been defined as a leisure activity (mental or physical in its manifestations) which is undertaken primarily for the attainment of amusement or pleasure. In reality play has few other obvious objectives until it is used for pedagogic purposes or to diffuse tension in a group. The great thing about play as far as street soccer is concerned is the fact that it tends to create an environment that is most conducive for learning:

1. Engagement with a particular activity
2. Freedom from stresses and other distractions
3. The possibility of simulating abstract concepts

Another wonderful benefit of play is the fact that it requires and fosters creativity. There is a reason why Google has consistently advocated for the use of play in the creative process. It is the activity that keeps people relaxed while at the same time giving them a means for experimentation. Normally play is a relatively judgement-free zone since people are not necessarily worried about winning or losing in a competitive sense. The taking part is as good as the token prizes at the end of the day.

Remember that trying out things during play is one of the ways in which the neurons are kept active and sharp. It is almost as if our mind is being taken to the gym and building the mental muscle that will keep it fit during our sporting careers and beyond. We develop what is known as movement intelligence and that in turn allows us to handle different situations no matter how unexpected the conditions are. In the next chapter we will look at how we nurture creativity through participation.

SUMMARY

- We need both intrinsic and extrinsic motivation in order to sustain our interest in the things we do. Coaches must therefore identify positive factors that contribute to the enjoyment of the sport while at the same time encouraging the natural interest of the individual in the activity at hand.

- Trust builds confidence which in turn translates into performance. Coaches must be able to earn the trust of their players as well as approach the sessions in a judgement-free mindset so as to put the learner at ease. They must also remain consistently supportive regardless of the short-term results. In the long run coaches are expected to help correct faults.

- Play is a great tool for keeping people relaxed and focused as they learn new things. It enables them to achieve the concentration and calm that is a prerequisite for deep learning. Coaches should therefore incorporate it into their routine as much as possible. It is an outlet for creativity and forces the participants to come up with innovative solutions to problems.

ACTIVE INVOLVEMENT AND NURTURING CREATIVITY

"A man not only needs to know how to fish, he needs to have the freedom to do it and a place to do it. That's where community comes in. We have to help each other..." Bill Ayers[8]

The need to improve the creativity of players has been almost universally acknowledged by most respectable sporting bodies including the FA. This is not only a good goal for any coach but also an aid in terms of achieving excellent results. Soccer is most exciting when it is memorable and unexpectedly revelatory. That does not mean that the fundamentals are necessarily forgotten; they are just reconfigured for a higher purpose. A coach should constantly question and evaluate their methodologies. One of the areas in which this can be done is to consider whether they are really on the right track when it comes to producing creative players. Creativity is really about developing new concepts, ideas, theories, methods and skills that bring value and meaning to the game.

The unpredictability of life on and off the pitch is one of the most compelling reasons for engaging the creativity framework that almost all of us are capable of. There are horizons

8   *(Rata, 2011)*

and insights in sport which we are not yet even aware of. However, through our creativity we can ensure that we are more than capable of meeting the challenges as they arise. We have been conditioned throughout our lives to deal with adversity and the unexpected. This is no different. The top-class players do not always have it their own way hence the need to train as if life will remain unpredictable. A coach has to develop their play in such a way that they remain exciting well into their career. Predictability of method and outcome is the death of exciting sport.

WHY CREATIVITY REMAINS SCARCE IN SPORT

As any coach will tell you, the vast majority of journeymen and journeywomen have one thing in common: they are not creative. Thus they trudge along in mediocrity particularly if they are earning just about enough to keep them in the sport. On the other hand there are players that will revolutionize an entire industry by their ways of thinking. They do not wait for things to happen but rather make things happen. Figure 7 shows how creativity, innovation and integrity can work together to create a complete player.

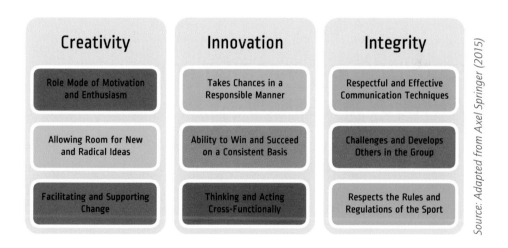

Creativity	Innovation	Integrity
Role Mode of Motivation and Enthusiasm	Takes Chances in a Responsible Manner	Respectful and Effective Communication Techniques
Allowing Room for New and Radical Ideas	Ability to Win and Succeed on a Consistent Basis	Challenges and Develops Others in the Group
Facilitating and Supporting Change	Thinking and Acting Cross-Functionally	Respects the Rules and Regulations of the Sport

Source: Adapted from Axel Springer (2015)

Figure 7: The Matrix of Creativity, Innovation and Integrity

It is easy to dismiss this as just a quirk of genes where some are born creative while others are not. Such an assumption would make coaching superfluous. Indeed all the literature tells us that the environment in which people live and work can significantly affect their level of creativity. In effect adversity, challenges, motivation and a supportive role by the coach help give birth to creativity.

Although what you are born with is very important in sport, what you learn along the way is equally (if not more) important. There is a reason why the winning teams spend billions of dollars on trainers, coaches and managers. They know that players need to be developed in a systematic way that pays attention to their individual needs. This is the kind of investment that any good coach will continuously make with regards to their wards, students or learners. Although teaching creativity may be too abstract for many coaches, they can create or recreate an environment in which it thrives. Let it develop, feed it and allow it to be expressed in the game. Normally the modalities of achieving this kind of environment border on laissez-faire coaching. In effect we begin to trust the learner to make their own mistakes and find their own solutions. That is a very radical step for many people and they prefer to shy away from it hence the scarcity of creativity in this most creative of sports.

RECOGNIZING THE FACT THAT NOT EVERYBODY IS A GENIUS

Your beloved learner is not always going to be a Ronaldo or a Beckham. They might be just another club soccer player that is trying to make it in this tough environment. You should be mature enough as a coach to do the best that you can without damaging the learner. It is not about just leaving the student to do as they please and hoping that they will eventually figure it out. Rather you are at the forefront of creating the right environment which allows that student to prosper in whatever they are doing. Sadly the current educational systems are just too rigid to take into account these needs. Therefore athletes end up being frustrated all the time by the seeming lack of support they receive from their coaches. Figure 8 shows how the coach and learner can achieve synchronicity through communication.

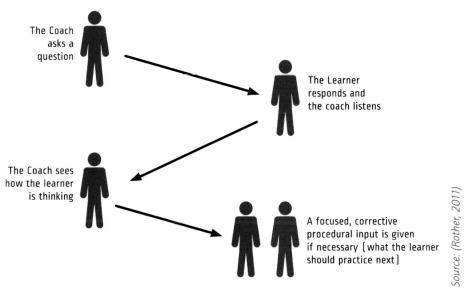

Figure 8: Achieving Coach-Learner Synchronicity

That is precisely where active engagement comes into play. By allowing the athlete to explore the learning process with the coach, acquiring knowledge and skills becomes second nature to them. The coach sows the seeds of motivation by introducing the player to interesting methods and techniques. They encourage them when things do not seem to make sense at first. Later on they start demanding very high-quality output as a consequence of everything that has been learned. Coaches need to avoid a situation where "we spend the first twelve months of our children's lives teaching them to walk and talk...the next twelve telling them to sit down and shut up."[9] Do not purge creativity from sport by trying to obsessively control the development of your players.

---

9   *Phyllis Diller as quoted by Young (2011, p. 55)*

THE FREEDOM TO EXPERIMENT AND MAKE MISTAKES

It is virtually guaranteed that the person you are coaching is going to mess up at some point. This is no surprise and you should be prepared for it. When we are young we know that we are going to fall and hurt ourselves. It is inevitable. Therefore we do not stop doing what we are doing just because we have made one mistake. Encourage your players to recover from the most career-threatening experiences. They do this through experimentation and having the confidence of knowing that they will eventually make it regardless of what the current challenges are. Players that are constantly micro-managed stop pushing the boundaries once they realize that no support is going to come from their coach on this front. Instead they always opt for the safest ways and means. It is that tenacity that allowed Thomas Edison to recover from 10,000 failed attempts before inventing the common light bulb.

For the uninitiated, street soccer can seem like chaos in action but we can assure you that there is a method to the madness. We believe that by creating unpredictability for players, we inspire them to innovate. Our judgement-free learning environments allow them to try out the alternatives without feeling as if they are the worst failure that has ever happened. Ultimately this is what is involved when valuing people. That is why "street soccer is for everyone who refuses to let their individuality, creativity and imagination die."[10] In the next chapter we will consider how the logical and illogical aspects of play can help us in our coaching duties.

---

10   *Darren Laver (Founder of the International Street Soccer Association)*

SUMMARY

🏃 We are all born with a certain amount of creativity. The experiences we get in life—including exposure to coaching—will help to take away the barriers that tend to hold back our natural creativity.

🏃 Making mistakes is not only natural but also necessary in order to improve the way in which we do things. An effective coaching environment is one which accepts this notion and allows players to experiment as much as possible. It therefore helps them make new discoveries and effectively innovate.

🏃 Street soccer creates a learning environment that is based on the following principles:

    🏃 We encourage all our players to try out things and make up their minds about them.

    🏃 We use play to increase enjoyment in the activity.

    🏃 Our coaching system deliberately promotes chaos in order to stimulate the naturally experimental natures of our learners.

USING THE LOGICAL NONSENSE THAT IS PLAY

"Play is the beginning of knowledge." George Dorsey[11]

Albert Einstein once described play as being the highest form of research. On the face of it, such an assertion may appear ridiculous since we have always associated playing with leisure activities that have absolutely nothing to do with learning. However, the reality is that play is a wonderful instrument in the hands of a seasoned coach. For example it can diffuse tension, re-engage bored athletes and introduce new concepts to the group. Play has often been cited as one of the great inspirations for creativity. Ironically it is the very frivolous nature of play that is its strongest weapon when it comes to creating judgement-free learning zones. The players do not feel as if they are under any pressure to win any particular game. Here the mere fact that they participate at all is a major achievement. Figure 9 shows an example of a comprehensive player development program that really incorporates play at the very beginning in order to introduce youngsters to complex concepts.

---

11   *(US Play Coalition, 2011)*

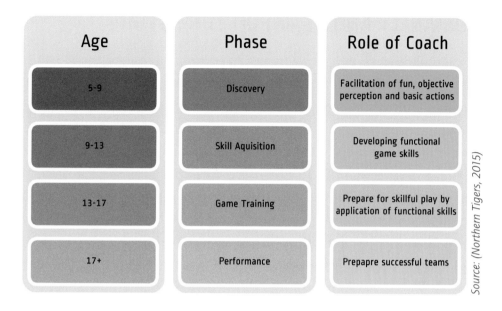

Age	Phase	Role of Coach
5-9	Discovery	Facilitation of fun, objective perception and basic actions
9-13	Skill Aquisition	Developing functional game skills
13-17	Game Training	Prepare for skillful play by application of functional skills
17+	Performance	Prepapre successful teams

Source: (Northern Tigers, 2015)

Figure 9: The Northern Tigers Player Development Program

As human society has advanced, we have forgotten the things that sparked creative thinking in our ancestors, people who survived lifestyles that are markedly more challenging than our own today. The same can be said of animals like lions who are able to achieve peak levels of conditioning and can easily outrun a human being. Interestingly all those life skills that make animals such dangerous opponents are started during play. Indeed human children today engage in horseplay, sometimes to the chagrin of over-protective parents. These principles can work very well in different contexts including sports. Soccer is a particularly contact-centered discipline which requires the actual physical application of the concepts that have been learnt. In that sense, play remains a very powerful tool for both the player and the coach despite the fact that some view it as a frivolous activity.

HUMANITY AND PLAY FOR THE FUTURE

It is acknowledged that athletes need to be fully engaged in an activity before they can really excel at it. Even those that are blessed with endless talents will need some kind of training in order to make the most of their gifts. Eduardo Chaves, one of the leading voices in soccer, argues that we need "creative improvisation, freedom, challenge, the union of passion and talent."[12] This ultimately results in fun, one of the most attractive aspects of soccer as we know it. Chaves argues for a thinking mindset that does not merely engage in robotic physical actions. We must therefore use the entire body and all of our brain in order to achieve the best that we can from the sport. This seems like a very logical response to an environment which is constantly changing. It is a reflection of the need to survive regardless of the conditions.

The coach, as a leader, mentor and elder, has a critical role to play in terms of inspiring the young athlete and also ensuring that they create an environment that supports effective learning. Not only do they provide stimulating environments but they also emphasize supportive relationships on which the young soccer player can rely at the most difficult points of their training. Society in general has to rethink its attitudes toward play as a pedagogic tool. It allows the interplay between adults and children whereby both sides get an insight into life after engaging in play. A case in point of the practical benefits of play is that of Rene Theophile Hyacinthe Laënnec (1781–1826) who was inspired to invent the stethoscope after watching two young boys attempt to send messages to one another using a piece of wood and a pin. Of course a judgement-free environment is a prerequisite for creating such a creative space.

---

12   (Chaves, 2013)

USING PLAY TO CREATE A COMPLETE PLAYER

One of the most important fruits of deliberate play is the creation of players who are complete in terms of their physical, technical and psychological performance. Individuals learn invaluable social skills such as speech and communication during play. They also develop certain mechanical skills that would otherwise be boring to acquire. Playing a fun game is certainly a lot better than repeating drills to distraction. Play can also trigger deep brain learning in terms of immersion, relaxed alertness and simulation. Street soccer does not attempt to make the job of the coach redundant; rather it seeks to add to the richness of the entire process. There is still room for practicing drills and technical skills but these must be balanced by new, intriguing additions to the routine. There is such a thing as over-coaching and that must be avoided. Figure 10 shows the six steps that are necessary for effective coaching without over-working the learner.

1 Motivation

· Motivation
· Persistence
· Arousal
· Social

2 Basic Movement

· Twist and Run
· Run
· Jump
· Stop and Start

3 Physical Fitness

· Endurance
· Mobility
· Strength
· Speed

4 Individual Ball Techniques

· Dribbling
· Ball Striking
· Receiving
· Striking

5 Group Skill

· Mobility versus Balance
· Penetration versus Display
· Depth versus Depth
· Width versus Concentration

6 Team Skill

· Co-Operative
· Confident
· Application of Strategy and Tactics
· Competitive

Source: (Itsagoal, 2013)

Figure 10: The Six Levels of Learning in Soccer

The way to look at it is to consider the fact that there is lots of untapped potential in the player. Without play, all this talent is wasted. It is not about creating anarchy and hoping for brilliance at the end of it; it is a balancing act of practice, drills, theory, physio and play. Furthermore the introduction of play can completely alter the tenor of the session for the better. Suddenly the athlete looks forward to practice instead of dreading mundane routines. The dichotomy of wrong and right answers has been rightly condemned for curtailing self-expression but we have to remember that players too can self-express. They may not use words but their ball-play will do the talking. Practice has been associated with drudgery but that need not be the end of the learning process. The coach must summon all the resources and put them toward getting a much better outcome.

REVISITING THE CONCEPTS OF CREATIVITY IN PLAY

We already know that human beings need to be stretched in order to perform at optimum capacity. By and large, they enjoy challenges. At the same time their curiosity is often limited to a few things that have a particular pull for them hence the need for persuasive pedagogical processes. People also need confidence in order to try out things. All these are the building blocks of creativity because they address the environmental restrictions that sometimes lead us to ignore the inherent creativity that we are born with. Although sports psychology sounds very complex and inaccessible, what it is trying to do is to tap into the mental resources of the athlete and get them to perform accordingly. Play is able to achieve the same objective because it is not only physical but also has a lot of thinking parts to it. By using flow states, the learning zone and peak performance as conceptual foundations of play, coaches are able to construct a player with a huge set of skills. The end product is a player with flair.

The implementation of a radical strategy is always frightening, particularly for the junior coaches who are so worried about doing the right things all the time. Thus the coaching session becomes nothing more than dribbling in and out with straight lines as well as the standard moves. This is a good way to get basic skills but if you want flair and creativity, you have to do a lot more. For example they need to learn how to move an opponent in order to create space. This is something that is learned through practice and being prepared to deal with unexpected responses from the other player.

SUMMARY

🏃 Human beings remain playful. It therefore makes sense to make use of our inherent nature and humanity when coaching. Play is one of the more effective ways of arousing the curiosity of athletes so that they can continue to engage in innovative strategies. Play is a very useful way of training someone to prepare for dealing with yet unseen problems.

🏃 Players who have passion will be able to make the best use of their talents. Flair allows them to create an original style that is not only entertaining but gives them a competitive advantage on the pitch. Coaches facilitate the acquisition of this capability through the provision of stimulating learning environments and a supportive network of relationships. Street soccer strives to achieve these objectives by adding interest to the traditional methods.

🏃 The brain learns through immersion, relaxed alertness and simulation. This is the foundation of most coaching programs and it is what street soccer has adopted as the backbone to our training ethos. We prefer this approach to the 10,000-hour rule which is eventually negatively affected by the laws of diminishing returns. Training is not just about quantity but also the qualitative elements.

🏃 In order to achieve the flow states element of creativity, the coach must ensure that there is a challenge that sufficiently stretches the capabilities of the student. In addition they must create interest in the activity at hand while at the same time building the self-confidence of the learner. This makes it easier for the learner to take calculated risks without necessarily being petrified by the possibility of failure.

CHAPTER 6

USING THE SOCRATIC METHOD IN SOCCER

"Education is the kindling of a flame, not the filling of a vessel." Socrates[13]

The merits of the current education system (no matter how flawed it may be) should not be underestimated. This is the pedagogic framework that has taken humanity through the Industrial Age, one of the most productive periods of all time. Nevertheless we have to recognize, embrace and adjust to the post-industrial age. The predetermined and static occupations of yesterday are slowly dying out and being replaced by creative industries. Sir Ken Robinson has been one of the leading critics of the current education system, precisely because it tends to control learners through targets, stifling their ability to think imaginatively. Meanwhile the world continues to evolve and definitely demands a multiplicity of intelligences which learners are often trained to suppress in favor of earning high scores on qualitative tests. Soccer has not survived some of the effects of this approach particularly given the prevalence of physical education as a co-curricular activity in most public schools.

---

13 *(Pychyl, 2008)*

Although the Socratic method was conceptualized centuries ago, it seems to have incredible relevance as we design responses for the new world and adjust our understanding of education as a whole. This method is based on a specific type of questioning which, if applied correctly, will create a student that is able to think for themselves and handle virtually any problem that life throws at them. Human beings are not empty vessels into which we pump information with the expectation that that information will be reproduced wholesale. They are individuals with characteristics that distinguish them from one another. This diversity of perspectives is what really requires a rich education that accounts for the quirks that make us interesting. By really thinking about the way in which people learn, we are able to offer learners opportunities and options that were previously beyond their reach.

CRITICAL THINKING AND ADVANCED PROBLEM SOLVING

Under the Socratic questioning paradigm, the teacher asks questions but not to just get preset and rehearsed answers (see Figure 11). Instead these questions are designed to provoke the learning into a higher level of thinking and analysis. They make the learner think about what is really going on so that they can begin to find ways of filling the gaps. Once the system is applied correctly, the learner will develop a deep understanding of the subject. They will also be able to apply its principles in various scenarios that may not be necessarily directly related. Learners then take full charge of the learning process as well as their own thought process. They can critically examine their responses to problems as well as their understanding of concepts. This type of questioning empowers learners by giving them the tools that they need in order to find solutions.

A Socratic teacher tends to put a lot of faith in their students; they believe that they can learn and implement what they have learned. This is not a situation where mollycoddling is acceptable, but it takes a lot of courage to overcome the institutional tendency to control learners. It is very different from the transmission model which works on a garbage-in-garbage-out framework. In soccer, the Socratic coach helps athletes gather

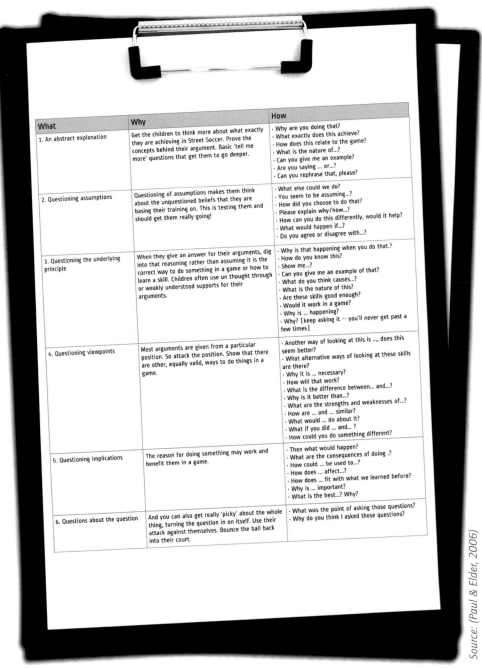

What	Why	How
1. An abstract explanation	Get the children to think more about what exactly they are achieving in Street Soccer. Prove the concepts behind their argument. Basic 'tell me more' questions that get them to go deeper.	· Why are you doing that? · What exactly does this achieve? · How does this relate to the game? · What is the nature of...? · Can you give me an example? · Are you saying ... or...? · Can you rephrase that, please?
2. Questioning assumptions	Questioning of assumptions makes them think about the unquestioned beliefs that they are basing their training on. This is testing them and should get them really going!	· What else could we do? · You seem to be assuming...? · How did you choose to do that? · Please explain why/how...? · How can you do this differently, would it help? · What would happen if...? · Do you agree or disagree with...?
3. Questioning the underlying principle	When they give an answer for their arguments, dig into that reasoning rather than assuming it is the correct way to do something in a game or how to learn a skill. Children often use un thought through or weakly understood supports for their arguments.	· Why is that happening when you do that.? · How do you know this? · Show me...? · Can you give me an example of that? · What do you think causes...? · What is the nature of this? · Are these skills good enough? · Would it work in a game? · Why is ... happening? · Why? [keep asking it -- you'll never get past a few times]
4. Questioning viewpoints	Most arguments are given from a particular position. So attack the position. Show that there are other, equally valid, ways to do things in a game.	· Another way of looking at this is ..., does this seem better? · What alternative ways of looking at these skills are there? · Why it is ... necessary? · How will that work? · What is the difference between... and...? · Why is it better than...? · What are the strengths and weaknesses of...? · How are ... and ... similar? · What would ... do about it? · What if you did ... and... ? · How could you do something different?
5. Questioning implications	The reason for doing something may work and benefit them in a game.	· Then what would happen? · What are the consequences of doing .? · How could ... be used to...? · How does ... affect...? · How does ... fit with what we learned before? · Why is ... important? · What is the best...? Why?
6. Questions about the question	And you can also get really 'picky' about the whole thing, turning the question in on itself. Use their attack against themselves. Bounce the ball back into their court.	· What was the point of asking those questions? · Why do you think I asked those questions?

Source: (Paul & Elder, 2006)

Figure 11: Six Types of Socratic Questions

their thoughts and skills so that they can organize them in a structure that works for them. Even where the skills are seemingly disparate, the learner will be able to combine them for the purpose of improving their knowledge, skills and performance. This is exactly how street soccer unleashes the full potential of its learners.

Here the ideas are never taught directly but rather teased out of the student. The questions are thought-provoking in the best sense of the phrase. It is a form of active learning which stimulates the young mind. In fact this type of critical thinking is really the purest form of intelligence that we can develop in sport. The difference between a sport like soccer and other academic disciplines is the fact that sports require doing as a follow-up to thinking. In such a scenario memorization on its own would be superfluous because the Socratic student thinks for themselves. They do not just parrot what they have been told or read.

ACCESSING MULTIPLE INTELLIGENCES FOR COACHING

We have generally moved away from the notion that an intelligent person is only so because they can pass academic exams. The vast majority of existing literature acknowledges the complexity of intelligence well beyond mere academic grades. Howard Gardner has tackled this topic in his book Frames of Mind: The Theory of Multiple Intelligences. It is a seminal piece of work which establishes eight critical aspects of intelligence. The corresponding abilities are represented in Figure 12. After further research, Gardener added existential and moral intelligence to the first eight. The remarkable thing about these intelligences is the fact that they call for the engagement of all the five human senses (sight, smell, hearing, touch and sound) in order to enrich the experience of playing soccer. Street soccer looks for this type of diverse collection of competencies as the best route toward becoming a complete player.

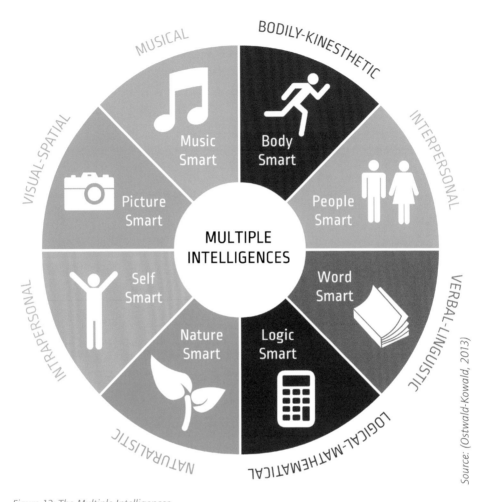

Figure 12: The Multiple Intelligences

Source: (Ostwald-Kowald, 2013)

Under the paradigm of multiple intelligences, it is possible to understand that information or knowledge is diverse and dynamic. Its multiplicity also makes it malleable and applicable to different situations. By that same token it is adaptable and adaptive. This is the semi-asymptotic approach to learning that is so effective in contact sports where one single skill is not enough to push someone to the next level. The engagement of all these intelligences also plays a role in developing our brain power because the neurons are constantly having to use different capabilities in order to get the desired results. The various linkages are what distinguishes the standard players from the truly extraordinary athletes that we often see on the world stage.

Intelligence is both dynamic and diverse, malleable and multiple, adaptive and, in a manner, asymptotic. Sparked neurons in our brains create various networks and linkages.

THE SENSITIVE AND RESPONSIVE COACH

As coaches, we need to understand that there is a limit to the amount of information that an individual can process at a given time. Therefore there is no point in demanding that all the various types of intelligences and learning techniques are simultaneously applied in one sitting. That would lead to a brain freeze! What we need is the ability to incorporate each of these elements in the overall learning program so that they are introduced at various stages. The learner may not even be aware that over the course of the training they have actually accessed all the intelligences that are available. We also need to be wary of following coaching dogma that has been handed down from generation to generation. This is the kind of situation that calls for imagination not only from the learner but also the coach. Mass-produced athletes have no flair and they bore the audiences to death.

The types of intelligence that will appear time and again during coaching sessions include:

- Bodily-kinesthetic (touch)

- Musical-rhythmic (sound)

- Visual-spatial (sight)

According to the International Street Soccer Association (ISSA), the three senses above are critical to understanding the nature of soccer skills. On the other hand the coach must also be humble enough to accept the fact that they will not always have all the answers. Therefore they have to engage in a kind of consultation with the athlete that they are looking after. In fact if the coaching is very successful then the learner may begin to find the right answers even without the overt participation of the coach.

STREET SOCCER

These are all natural instincts. The coach is not doing anything that is going to warp the student. On the contrary, they are tapping into what comes to the student naturally in order to get the best results. In a world where the attention span of virtually everyone is shrinking, Socratic questioning forces the athlete to really think about what they are doing. This is something that models such as Long-Term Player Development (LTAD) developed by Istvan Balyi have failed to do. They do not acknowledge differences and are therefore prone to employing the right strategy to the wrong learner. Those children that have managed to remain creative despite the stifling conditions must be admired for their resilience. On the other hand coaches must find better ways of reaching the full talents of their wards. We conclude this book with a chapter that considers how the street soccer games actually work in light of all the things that we have discussed so far.

SUMMARY

- The traditional models of education are no longer responsive to the creativity of the modern age. Therefore they must be improved through the Socratic method. Coaches should focus on what allows natural intelligence and creativity to prosper. To that end, athletes should be exposed to as many diverse experiences as possible in order to learn the art and science of managing unpredictability.

- The starting point for a creative education is understanding the human instinct and how it is in tune with revolutionary ideas about pedagogy. Human beings learn best when they are allowed to think for themselves. True education therefore does not provide answers for parroting but rather inspires the learner to explore all that is around them in a meaningful way.

- The intelligence of a learner is not limited to their ability to pass academic exams. It encompasses such diverse elements including visual-spatial, logical-mathematical, musical-rhythmic, interpersonal, bodily-kinesthetic, naturalist and intrapersonal skills. Sports normally access touch, sound and sight as the go-to skills for most matches. That is where the coach should focus because they touch on the innate learning tools of sport.

The coach best helps learners by planning a program that is capable of eliciting the best that their talents can offer. This may take on the form of experimentation or adding challenges that bring out the best in the athlete. Not all the activities can be done in one movement so it is important to schedule these learning activities using comprehensive and diverse methodologies so that the learner attains a full education.

OVERVIEW OF STREET SOCCER GAMES

"Too often coaches give players answers to remember rather than problems to solve. Our sessions are therefore characterized by randomness, variety, challenge, decisions, choices and problem-solving." Dan Micciche[14]

When we talk of organized chaos in street soccer, some readers are confused. They cannot reconcile the profound differences between being chaotic and being organized. Although these diametrically opposed concepts do not appear to sit well as a team at first glance, they are actually critical in developing the model that is street soccer. Here one has to consider that organization is where the first team is determined to avoid giving away goals. They structure their activities and positioning in such a way as to achieve this objective. Chaos is then brought in by the opposing team whose job is to disrupt any plans that have been made, thereby ensuring that they score as much as possible. It is this duality of objectives that gave birth to the concept of organized chaos.

Unlike some sports, soccer does not have rigid rules which determine the flow of the game. It is far from predictable and that is one of the reasons why the scoring rate is

---

14   (Micciche, 2015)

much lower than in, say, basketball. The players are constantly on the move which allows for a certain level of randomness. Yes, there are set pieces and formations as part of the game plan but these are not guaranteed to succeed given the fluidity of strategy that is inherent within soccer. The coach has to develop creative players because they are the ones that have the best opportunity to score in this unpredictable game. Indeed these creative players are often the ones that are responsible for creating the opportunities in the first place. The Holy Grail of street soccer is the creative attacker. This type of soccer player is difficult to defend against and that is precisely why coaches spend a lot of money to develop this particular type of skill set.

ASSISTING PLAYERS TO BECOME CREATIVE ATTACKERS

The first thing to realize is that the other team will try to stop, slow down or even distract anyone that appears to be on the attack. During player development, this possibility should be explored so that the athlete is not startled by any sneaky defensive moves by the other side. In fact those who really love soccer enjoy the challenge of being able to penetrate difficult defenses. It is a validation of all the work that they have put in so far. Players should be given the freedom to experiment and improvise; the soccer ball itself is an extension of their self-expression. They start by knowing the attack zones as well as the overall set runs and movements so that their creativity will not conflict with the other members of the team.

Once those rules have been fully understood, the player will be encouraged to look for the most optimal ways of achieving the cardinal goals of soccer: to score without conceding goals. It has become something of a downer on the sport that many coaches like to integrate synchronization into the training sessions. This is not the right way to go about building a team. What you need is a set of intelligent and courageous players who are totally unpredictable to their opponents but work in a complementary fashion with their teammates. It is better to guide the players without insisting that they have to behave in exactly the same way. Street soccer does not ignore the fundamentals of soccer; it merely encourages the use of creativity when implementing them. Remember that if you rely on set pieces all the time, the other side will soon catch on to your patterns and predict where you are going before you even arrive. That is a dangerous place to be in a competitive match.

We keep talking about improvisation but it is not that easy to pull off. The players must learn to boldly create confusion in the other team by doing unexpected things. The attacking play must be relentless. All this will arise if the diligent coach has been gradually introducing the method in the training sessions. With time, all the players will become comfortable with making split-second decisions and executing them with flair. The other members of the team will also learn to fall in line so as to ensure that the team scores. Street soccer recommends a progressive system which starts with a rigorous foundation on which fluency is eventually built. Based on the selected strategic formation, the players are still able to creatively make rapid individual decisions and yet gel together as a team when it comes to objectives.

HARNESSING THE POWER OF CHAOS

In truth, soccer is rather chaotic at the best of times. Although we talk about the beautiful game, what we are really referring to is the individual style of the players rather than the spectrum of two teams desperately trying to score while defending. This is why decisions are made in an instant but can affect the rest of the game. Adaptability is a very valuable commodity in this game. It is what separates the true players from those that just make up the numbers. Indeed those teams that are able to quicken the pace of the game like the Brazilian national team will cause unprepared opponents to commit so many unforced errors because they are not used to making such quick significant decisions all the time. It takes a very clever and experienced player to pull this off well. What coaches do is to ensure that they simulate the chaos in practice so that the players are not fazed by it when they encounter the real thing.

The beauty of working with street soccer games is that you get to recreate this chaos in a fun way so that practice is always associated with positive feelings. The games that we use are designed to access different stimulus points for players. Interestingly, this multiplicity of stimuli also encourages the players to learn how to control the ball. At the same time the players are able to improve their balance and coordination. The pressurized and confusing nature of the training environment means that the players learn the importance of accuracy and efficiency during shot selection. The players are also able to broaden their overall range through street soccer so that they become multi-skilled members of the teams that they later join.

SOME STREET SOCCER GAMES TO TRY OUT

We have selected 50 great soccer games (25 small-sided games and 25 1-v-1 games) which you can try out with your players in order to implement all the great practices in this book. They can be used in the coaching sessions with most ages and abilities. We seek to challenge the players' talents and abilities so that they can aim even higher in areas such as tactics, technical proficiency, mental acumen, psychological resilience, socialization and physical endurance. These games are original and are designed by Darren Laver and Gareth Long with the express purpose of improving coaching techniques and outcomes. We have designed them so that they place your athletes in realistic situations that motivate and stimulate them. Ultimately these games are enjoyable and memorable while challenging the powers of all players who participate in them. We are trying to get players to experiment and try new things in order to make the game that much more interesting. Of course we are also aware that good technique leads to excellent results and glory for the team. These games are very adaptable and should be incorporated into your training schedule to suit the individual needs of the players.

THE COACH'S ROLE IN THE SMALL-SIDED GAMES: 20 TOP TIPS

1. Plan and recognize the technical, tactical, physical, social and psychological skills that each of the games will help develop.

2. Have a range of variations, options and progressions to help and challenge players to be successful.

3. Have a range of variations, options and progressions to help keep the players motivated and the games stimulating.

4. Consider and plan for individual challenges for certain players to try within the game.

5. Allow and encourage players to make choices and suggest changes.

6. Allow and encourage players to try things, take risks and to make mistakes.

7. Give players time to plan and discuss strategies and tactics.

8. Use 'time-outs' when appropriate to allow players to evaluate.

9. Consider and vary how teams are chosen (e.g. friends, random, birthdays...)

10. Don't worry about uneven teams (e.g. 6v5).

11. Consider and vary the pitch shapes/sizes.

12. Allow players time to get used to rules and constraints and to solve problems themselves.

13. Don't worry if it looks 'messy'.

14. Offer help/advice when needed or asked for.

15. Avoid 'jumping in' on every mistake.

16. Avoid stopping play and all players to make a coaching point too often.

17. Make sure players play in different positions and in different teams.

18. Ask questions which promote dialogue between players, and between you and the players. (See Chapter 5)

19. Praise effort, good ideas, trying stuff, skill, sportsmanship, being a good team-mate...

20. Always think "how can I make this better next time".

1-V-1 SOCCER GAMES

Developing Players' Abilities to Attack and Defend in 1-v-1 Situations

1 V 1 RACE

Setup

🏃 In the middle of the pitch, place two cones per player and two soccer balls.

🏃 Players have their own base in which they will place cones.

🏃 Two goalkeepers defend a goal each.

How It Works

1. On a command, all four players run, collect a cone from the middle, return to their base and repeat so they have two cones in their base. Players may pick up any cones.
2. The first player back into the middle of the area steals one of the balls and decides which goal to attack.
3. The second player steals the remaining ball and attacks the other goal.
4. The two remaining players become defenders and try to stop the other players from scoring.
5. Players keep count of how many goals they score.

Options, Progressions and Variations

Use balls instead of cones; players must dribble the balls back to their base.

Players who have more goals are given the challenge of starting from the back of their base or from a sitting position.

If defenders regain the ball, they can attack the other goal.

Have just one ball in the middle; the first player to get the ball passes to a player of their choice to initiate a 2-v-2 game.

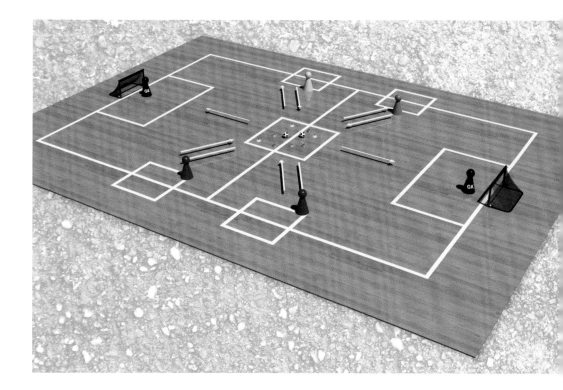

1 V 1 TO 3 V 3

Setup

- Organize a pitch with a series of small goals at each end.

- Players face an opponent ready for a 1-v-1 game.

How It Works

1. The game starts by a player passing to their 1-v-1 opponent to initiate the attack.
2. Players play a 1-v-1 game but can score in ANY of the goals on their opponent's line. As such, they must defend ALL the goals on their own line.
3. When a goal is scored, players then help any of their teammates still playing in order to make other combinations, like 2-v-2 or 2-v-1 games. So if two goals have been scored, a 3-v-3 game should take place.
4. Which team scores the most goals in each round?

Options, Progressions and Variations

- Players can't score in the goal they scored in previously.

- Use scoring zones and award more points for a goal scored closer to the goal to encourage players to take on their opponents.

- Players can't score with the same part of the foot two times in a row.

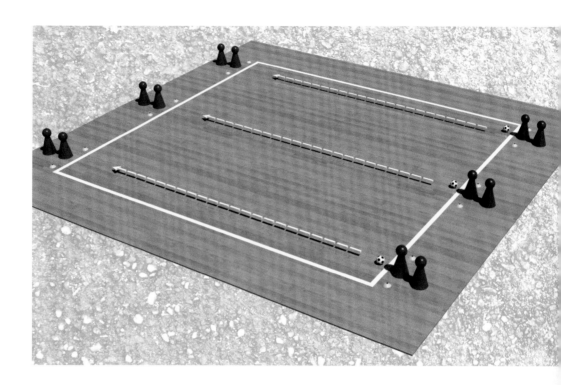

ATTACK ZONES

Setup

🏃 Organize a middle playing zone with four 1-v-1 areas in the end zone (attack zones).

🏃 In the middle zone, teams play 3-v-3 games (or add a floater to create an overload).

How It Works

1. The aim of the teams is to try and create an opportunity for one of the players to break out and play a 1-v-1 game against a defender, and to score by dribbling over the end line whilst staying in the defender's zone.

2. When this happens, the attacker has a set time limit to dribble over the line or they must leave the ball and retreat back to the middle zone.

3. If the defenders win back the ball, they play into the middle zone and the attacker recovers into the middle zone for the 3-v-3 game.

Options, Progressions and Variations

🏃 The defender may dribble into the middle zone, but they must be replaced by a teammate.

🏃 The attacker may move between the two end zones, but defenders cannot move zones.

🏃 If after a few seconds the 1-v-1 game is not successful, allow another attacker to enter the other attacking zone to make a 2-v-2 game.

ATTACK, DEFEND AND SAVE

Setup

🏃 Set up four 1-v-1 games plus goalkeepers as shown in the diagram.

🏃 Red players have one ball each; one other ball is kept in the middle of the diamond.

How It Works

1. The red players attack the blue defenders and try to score past the yellow goalkeepers.
2. If they score or miss or the blue defenders tackle, they then proceed to dribble the ball to the diamond, and the red player starts again.
3. How many goals can the red team score in a set period of time?
4. Teams rotate after a set period of time so all players get to attack, defend and be the goalkeeper.

Options, Progressions and Variations

🏃 Red players move around after 30 seconds to attack another goal; the game continues for four 30-second periods.

🏃 Allow the red players to attack a different goal at any time; they may leave their quarter, but the defenders may not. This will create overloads such as 2-v-1 games in some quarters.

🏃 If a blue player gets the ball into the diamond, he or she becomes the attacker straight away. The red player goes in the goal and the yellow players become the defenders.

At the coach's command, the attacking team immediately shoots at the goal; the attacking team then collects the ball that is placed in the middle of the pitch and plays a 4-v-4 game where both teams can score in any of the four goals.

BIB THROW

Setup

- Two teams play on a normal pitch with a goal each to defend and attack.

- Additional ways of scoring are also added (here corner goals are used).

- Balls are placed on the end lines of the pitch.

- Each player is paired up with a player from the opposition.

- The coach walks around the pitch holding a bib.

How It Works

1. The normal game starts with both teams trying to score in the center goals; each goal is counted.

2. At occasional intervals, the coach may pass the bib to any player. At that point the normal game carries on; however, the player who was given the bib quickly collects a ball from beside their goal (or on the side line) and attacks either of the corner goals at the opposite end. If they score, the goal counts toward their team's total. The paired player from the opposition has to react and try to stop them scoring. If they regain the ball they can attack the opposition's corner goals.

3. This 1-v-1 game within the normal game continues until a goal is scored or the ball goes off the pitch, at which point the ball is returned to its original place and both players rejoin the normal game.

4. Which team scores the most goals?

Options, Progressions and Variations

The coach can give out two bibs at once.

Vary the start positions of the 1-v-1 balls.

Allow the goalkeepers to defend the corner goals, as well as the center goals.

The coach carries a ball instead of a bib. When a player receives this ball from the coach they attack straight away, but any player from the opposition can react and stop them scoring.

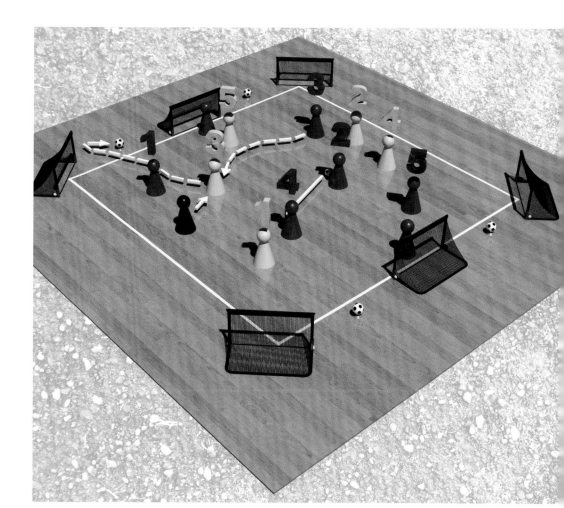

BREAKAWAY TO SCORE

Setup

- In a coned-off area, nine players (three reds, three blues and three yellows) pass a ball between their team (working on aspects like passing and receiving at pace, receiving between players and dribbling).

- A defender waits outside the area and protects the goalkeeper and goal.

How It Works

1. When the coach calls a color (e.g. yellow), the yellow player in possession of the ball at that time must leave the area and attack the goal. The other two yellow players must run around any cone before recovering to help the defender (creating a 1-v-3 game).

2. If yellow scores, they gain a point; if not, the yellows return quickly to the coned-off area.

3. The coach dictates the pace by how often they call out the colors.

4. Can the players (attacker, defender and goalkeeper) recognize the position of the recovery defenders and use it to their advantage?

Options, Progressions and Variations

- Recovery defenders cannot run around the same cone.

- Number the players within their colors. If yellow #1 attacks, then yellow #2 becomes an attacker and yellow #3 becomes a recovery defender (creating a 2-v-2 game rather than a 1-v-3 game).

Have another goal (with a defender and goalkeeper) at the other end and allow attackers to decide which goal they attack.

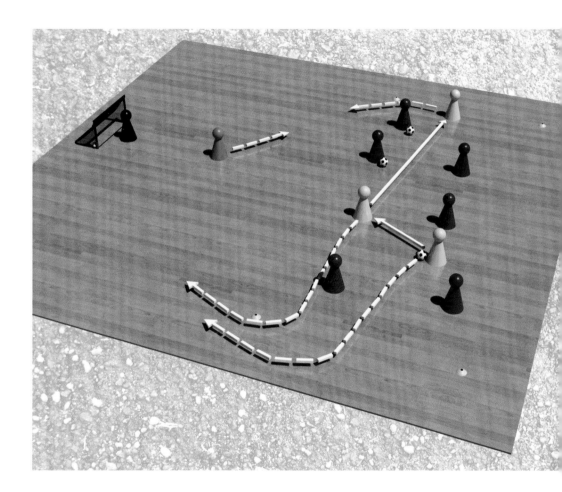

CENTER COURT CHAMPIONS

Setup

- Players pair up with another player and then go to courts 1 through 6 or to the center court.

- Each court has a different version of a 1-v-1 game.

- The timing of the games are controlled by what happens on center court.

How It Works

1. Players work on different skills with different activities at each court.
   - Court 1: A panna game with one ball; the blue and red players compete to see who can get the most pannas.
   - Court 2: This is a game of Line Ball; players try to stop the ball on the opposition's line.
   - Court 3: Which player can keep the ball up in the air the longest?
   - Court 4: This game is a normal game with small goals which can be scored in.
   - Court 5: This is a game of Corner Goals; each player attacks two goals.
   - Court 6: This is a game of Cone Knock-Down; each player has a cone which they attack and try to knock over with the ball.
   - Center court: This is a game of Head Tennis. If you don't have a net, then mark out a no-man's zone with four cones which the ball must clear. The game is first to six points (like a set in tennis). As soon as a player gets to six they shout "Winners!" and all the games on the other courts must stop.

2. All players then meet up in center court and grab a new partner. The coach picks two players to play on center court and the other players go off to one of the other courts for a new game. When everyone is set, the coach starts the new games.

3. Whenever a player wins a challenge, they get three points. A draw is worth two points and a defeat is worth one point.

Options, Progressions and Variations

🦵 This version caters to 14 players, but it works just as well as a doubles competition.

🦵 Each outside court plays the same game in each round (e.g. they all play the panna game first; Line Ball next, and so on).

🦵 Allow the players to choose which 1-v-1 version they play on the outside courts.

COLOR GOALS

Setup

🦶 Organize a pitch with three different colored goals at each end.

🦶 Each player HOLDS a bib which matches one of the colored goals.

🦶 The coach has two cones of each color and some balls.

How It Works

1. To start the game, the coach holds a cone in each hand (in the example they hold a yellow cone in their left hand and a red cone in their right hand). This works best if they pick up the cones from the floor.
2. This means that the player holding the yellow bib to the coach's left enters the pitch to play a 1-v-1 game against the player holding the red bib to the coach's right. The coach plays the ball onto the pitch.
3. The yellow player gains extra points for their team if they can score in the yellow goal (as shown) and the red player gains extra points if they can score in the red goal.

Options, Progressions and Variations

🦶 Behind the goals, players quickly swap and pass bibs until the coach holds up the cones. This version results in players having to attack different goals each time and react quickly to their new color.

🦶 Players cannot score in their colored goal. Can defenders recognize this and steer them away from the two remaining goals?

🦶 Each color equals a type of skill (e.g. yellow = panna; red = step over; green = flip flap). If the player can execute the skill before scoring in the correct goal, even more points are awarded.

🦶 At any point the coach can pick up another cone and that player can now join in to make a 2-v-1 game.

GAUNTLET DRIBBLE

Setup

- Divide the pitch into three separate areas and put one defender or guard in each area.

- The defenders in the first area have a ball at their feet that they have to keep under control.

- The defenders in the second area carry a tennis ball in their hands.

- The defenders in the final area are normal defenders.

- Attackers (yellow players) have a ball each and line up at an end line.

How It Works

1. The challenge for the attackers is to dribble through the three areas without getting caught. The challenge for the defenders is to stop them!

2. In the first area, defenders have to keep control of their own ball while trying to tag the attacker. Attackers try to keep away from the defender by changing direction to make the defender lose control of their own ball before escaping.

3. In the second area, defenders try to roll the tennis ball against the attacker's ball. The attackers manipulate their ball to tempt the defender into rolling the ball and then move past them.

4. In the third area, defenders try to gain possession of the attacker's ball and dribble it out of the area.

5. Attackers do not have to work in a straight line and can move diagonally into areas as shown in the diagram. At times they may look to enter areas where a 1-v-1 game is already happening, but players should be encouraged to challenge themselves.

6. If the defender is successful in stopping an attacker escape, they gain one point, as does the attacker if they are successful. Decide whether attackers carry on to the next area even if they do not beat the defender or whether they return to the start.
7. Rotate attackers and defenders regularly.

Options, Progressions and Variations

🏃 Use other 1-v-1 options within the areas (e.g. attackers carry a ball and defenders attempt to tag the ball; attackers have a bib as a tail and defenders try to grab it).

🏃 Use three goals and goalkeepers at the end of the area. Can attackers score a goal?

🏃 Have a variety of shapes—circles, triangles, rectangles—to provide different challenges.

🏃 Have one defender who dribbles a ball but who can operate in-between the areas (a la PacMan!) so attackers have to scan and decide where to go after leaving an area.

N-AND-OUT DRIBBLE

Setup

⫶ Organize a nine-square grid or similar as shown.

⫶ Place one defender in each square.

⫶ Place the rest of the players around the outside of the square with one ball each.

⫶ Around the perimeter of the square are some colored gates.

How It Works

1. Attacking players enter through a gate of their choice, and then have the challenge of trying to exit through a gate of the same color, while avoiding the defenders in the squares.
2. Defenders are locked in their square and not allowed out.
3. If the defender gains possession of the ball (e.g. gets two consecutive tackles on the ball), the other player must pick up their ball, run through a gate and try the challenge again.
4. How many times can the players achieve the challenge?
5. How many times did the defender make a player pick their ball up?
6. Can players keep their heads up and identify where gaps exist (e.g. an occupied defender)?
7. Do players go for an easier challenge or go for gates furthest away from each other?
8. Do players plan a route or do they respond to the changing pictures?
9. Change defenders after a set time period.

Options, Progressions and Variations

- If successful in the challenge, players score a point for every grid they passed through. See if players get in and out quickly or try to score more points.

- No more than two attackers are allowed in one square at any time.

- Allow defenders to cover two squares.

INTERCEPT

Setup

🏃 Inside an area, place small goals (pop up goals or gates work well).

🏃 Pair up the players so they will play a 1-v-1 game against an opponent.

🏃 Give each pair one ball.

How It Works

1. Let the yellow players start with the ball and the reds defend (you don't need bibs).
2. Yellow players must score in each goal or score eight times (if using eight goals) in a set time period.
3. Red players try to regain the ball off their opponent, and either pass the ball out of the area or try to panna their opponent or any other yellow player in 10 seconds. If they can do this, the yellow player panna'd has to go back to zero goals!
4. At the end of the set time period, how many goals has the yellow team scored?
5. Swap over teams and swap partners.

Options, Progressions and Variations

🏃 Have a floating player who can also tackle; at times players may be faced with a 1-v-2 situation.

🏃 Place goals around the outside of the area; if defenders regain the ball, they must try and pass into one of these goals.

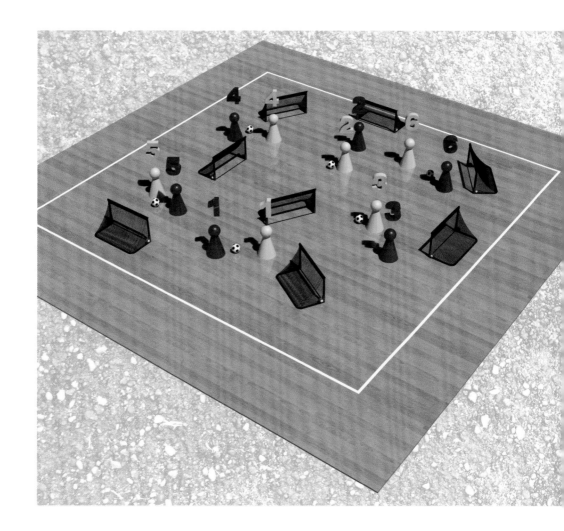

MIXED QUARTERS

Setup

🦶 Divide a small pitch into quarters and organize a 1-v-1 game in each area.

🦶 Three spare balls are placed along the line as shown.

How It Works

1. First game: Players compete in a 1-v-1 game (e.g. panna battle) in a quarter of the pitch. Winner gets a point.
2. Second game: At the coach's command, the balls being used are kicked in to the goals and two 2-v-2 games begin (e.g. teams try to dribble the ball over the line; players quickly get the ball on the dotted line to start the game). Winning players get a point.
3. Third game: At the coach's command, the balls being used in the 2-v-2 game are kicked in to the goals, and the players quickly get the ball placed in the middle of the pitch to start a 4-v-4 game (e.g., one goal to win; one-touch finish, reds v blues). Winning players get a point.
4. At this point the pitch is reset and players start over with a new partner.

Options, Progressions and Variations

Keep changing the 1-v-1, 2-v-2 and 4-v-4 games and practices in each section (e.g., the 1-v-1 game may be attacking a cone; the 2-v-2 game may be scoring in corner goals; the 4-v-4 game may be a game of head tennis).

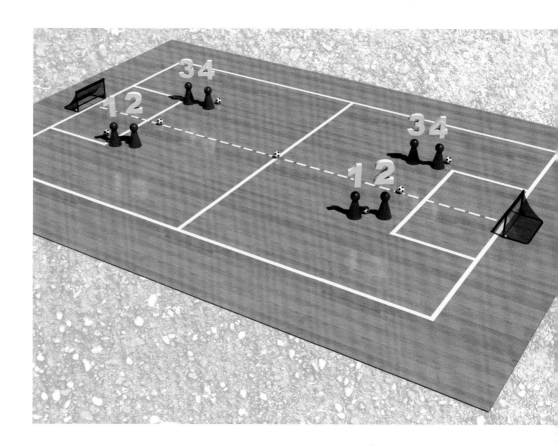

PANNA KNOCKOUT

Setup

This game is for two players, one ball and a small playing area with two small goals!

How It Works

1. Games last for a set time period (e.g. 3 minutes).
2. As in a usual game, the player who scores the most goals at the end of the time period would win, however...
3. If during the three minutes a player is able to panna their opponent, they win the game immediately, regardless of the score at the time.

Options, Progressions and Variations

⚽ Each player is provided with a skill card (e.g. step over, flip flap). If they can beat their opponent using that skill within three minutes, the game is over! Decide whether players know what their opponent's skill is.

⚽ Instead of finishing the game, a panna is worth three goals.

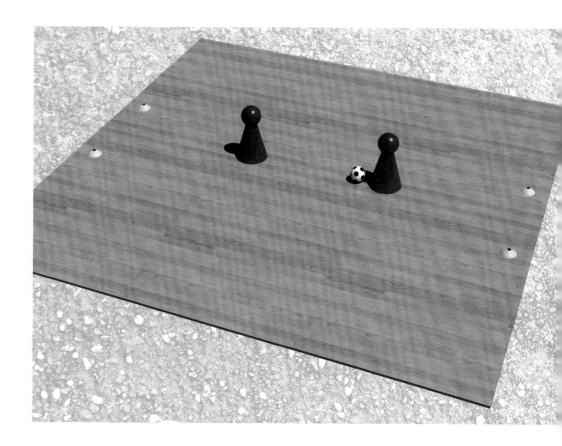

PENALTY BATTLE

Setup

🏃 Two teams set up for a penalty competition, but they each have a goal to shoot in to.

🏃 Another ball waits on the half-way line.

How It Works

1. At the coach's signal, both players strike their penalty. If they score, they earn a point for their team.
2. Whatever the outcome of their penalty, the same players immediately turn to gain control of the ball on the half-way line and play a 1-v-1 game in to the goals (each attacking the opposite goal to the one they took their penalty in). If they score in a set amount of time, they earn two points for their team.
3. After this, the next players take their turn.

Options, Progressions and Variations

🏃 After the penalties, the coach plays a ball in to one of the players to give them an advantage.

🏃 For more chaos, play into four goals and instead of a 1-v-1, it becomes a 2-v-2 or a 1-v-1-v-1-v-1 game.

🏃 Spread the waiting players around the area. If they are passed to by their teammate in the 1-v-1 part, they are released and join in; therefore, this could go up to a 5-v-5 game before the next penalty!

RELEASE THE TEAM

Setup

🦶 Set up two even teams, pair them off and place them around the pitch with one player standing behind the other (as shown).

🦶 Both teams have an allocated goalkeeper.

🦶 The coach has a series of balls ready to use.

How It Works

The coach plays a ball in to initiate a directional 1-v-1 game. If the balls goes off the pitch, instead of a throw-in, the player dribbles the ball into play to continue the 1-v-1 game. Both players may try to score.

A player also has the option to pass to one of their players AT THE FRONT OF THEIR TEAM'S LINE. So in the example shown, yellow #1 is able to pass to yellow #2, but would not have been able to pass to yellow #3 or #5.

Play continues in this way. So if the red player regains the ball, they have the option of passing to red #5, red #3, or red #2 (who is now at the front of the line).

The game continues until a goal has been scored. This could be at 1v1, 2v1, 2v2, 3v2, 3v3, 4v3, 4v4, 5v4 or 5v5, as you cannot have more than a one-player overload.

If goalkeepers save the ball, they can also release one of their players with accurate distribution.

Options, Progressions and Variations

🏃 Have a set time period in which an overload is allowed for. In the example shown, yellow #1 and #2 would have 20 seconds to score before red #2 may join in.

🏃 Every time the coach shouts "Change," the players in line swap places. This means the players in the pitch have to keep scanning to see which players can be released.

🏃 If you want to work on 1-v-1 skills, award more points (when a goal is scored) while teams are matched. If you want to work on passing and creating overloads, then award more points when a goal is scored while having an overload.

🏃 Award bonus points for scoring when playing against an overload.

🏃 Instead of having the players on the side of the pitch, have them on the pitch linked together like a chain; the chain must remain linked but can stop shots. They are released in the same way (via a pass) and that player then leaves the chain and joins in to make a 2-v-1 game.

🏃 For maximum chaos, play on a triangle pitch with three teams and lines of three.

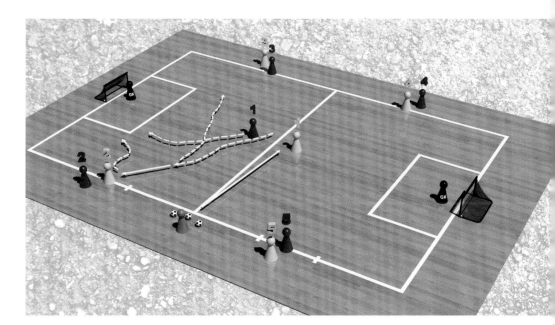

ROCK-PAPER-SCISSORS

Setup

Split the players into two teams. Half of each team start as defenders (and defend a goal each); the other half are attackers and begin inside the middle circle.

How It Works

1. Players pair off inside the circle and play a game of rock-paper-scissors.
2. Each winning player then takes the ball, leaves the circle and tries to escape through one of the goals (e.g. yellow player must try to dribble across the green goal). If they do, they score a goal for their team.
3. The defenders try to win the ball and pass it to one of their teammates inside the circle.
4. As soon as a player has someone from the opposite team to play against in the middle circle, a new game of rock-paper-scissors starts straight away. As a result, players should end up playing against different opponents throughout.
5. The coach does not need to control this and players should play as quickly as possible, trying to score as many goals in the set time.
6. Swap defenders and attackers after a set time.
7. Which team scores the most goals?

Options, Progressions and Variations

🔄 Allow players in the circle who lost rock-paper-scissors to help defend outside the circle (1-v-2 game).

🔄 Play with three teams, with one team being the defender for all the goals. The players in the circle can then attack any goal.

🔄 Instead of playing rock-paper-scissors in the middle, have another way of deciding which player gets to attack (e.g. a panna competition, which player can keep the ball up the most with their weaker foot).

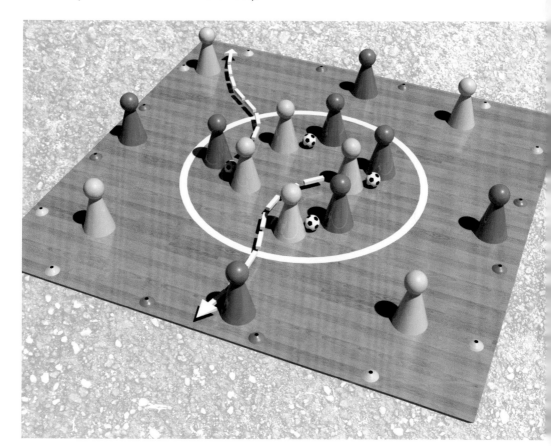

RYDER CUP COMPETITION

Setup

- Divide players into two teams (e.g. reds v yellows).

- Set up a number of pitches for 2-v-2 games.

How It Works

1. Both teams secretly divide their team into pairs and record this on a whiteboard (e.g.,the red team's whiteboard may look like this:
   - Pitch 1: Stu & Nick
   - Pitch 2: Sam & Jacob
   - Pitch 3: Joe & George
   - Pitch 4: Luis & Daniel
   - Pitch 5: Rich & Harvey
   - Pitch 6: Jamie & Jack

2. The yellow team will have divided their players without knowing what the red team has done (like in the Ryder cup).

3. When this is done all players go to the correct pitch and find out who their opponents are.

4. Short games (e.g. 2-3 minutes) are played; if a team wins, they earn a point for their team, with a draw worth a half of a point.

5. The scores are recorded on a master scoreboard and teams then re-select their pairs and the process resumes.

6. Players cannot play with the same partner for more than two games (or must always have a different partner). You may appoint a Ryder Cup captain to oversee the team's strategy.

7. Which team gains the most points after a set number of rounds?

Options, Progressions and Variations

• Each team has one or more players who can switch pitches whenever they like (shown in the diagram by the #13 players).

• Each pitch has different ways of scoring (e.g. corner goals, end line, balls on cones).

• Allow the teams to select a different number of players per pitch (e.g. a single player on one pitch and three players to another pitch) so that some games are likely to be uneven.

• Play 1-v-1 singles before moving on to the foursomes version.

SHOOT AND DRIBBLE

Setup

Organize two teams who face each other at the opposite end of a square.

The square is divided into a dribbling zone and a shooting zone.

Two goals are set up on the side of the square, with a cone facing them on the other side of the square.

How It Works

1. On the coach's command, the first red and yellow players in the line dribble as quickly as they can around the cone, across the square and enter the shooting zone.
2. As soon as they enter the shooting zone, they shoot to score against the opposition's goalkeeper.
3. They gain two points for their team from scoring first and one point just for scoring.
4. After shooting, the players quickly turn to defend back in the dribbling zone.
5. As soon as the first players enter the shooting zone, the next players in the line enter the dribbling zone and try to get across the square. The red player goes as soon as the yellow player enters the shooting zone and vice versa.
6. The red player who shoots tries to stop the yellow player dribbling across and the yellow shooter stops the red dribbler.
7. Players gain two points for being first across and one point just for getting across.

Options, Progressions and Variations

- Have players shoot diagonally into the other goal.

- If the players who have already shot regain possession of their opponent's ball, they can once again enter the shooting zone for a second shot.

Play with two goals placed at opposite ends of the square. When players have shot with their own ball, they turn, race to a ball in the middle and play a 1-v-1 game trying to score in the opposite goal from the one they have just shot at.

THE ONE-GOAL CHAOS TOURNAMENT

Setup

- Organize multiple pitches (four are shown) and multiple teams (24 players ready to play 1-v-1 games are shown). The more players and teams the better! Fast, quick games will result.

- Each pitch must have a waiting area for players and teams not playing. Don't worry—they won't be waiting long!

How It Works

Tournament Rules

1. Each game is over when one goal is scored.
2. The player or team that scores the goal gains one point. Players will need to keep count of their points as the tournament continues.
3. After a goal has been scored, BOTH players must leave the pitch and join the shortest queue ready for another game. Players from the original 1-v-1 game can join different queues.
4. A game can only begin when there are two players on the pitch. Begin with a pass from one player to their opponent.
5. At the end of a pre-determined period of time, players will have accumulated a score determined by the number of goals they have scored.

Encourage

- Players should be ready to play quickly, as more games equal more opportunities to score points.

⚽ It is also in the interest of waiting players to get the ball back in play quickly if it goes off the pitch.

⚽ Players should take risks since losing a game doesn't affect their points score (they will be playing again very soon); however, if their risk works they will have gained a point.

Options, Progressions and Variations

⚽ If using this format with teams (e.g. 2v2), try this rule:

⚽ After a goal all four players can join different queues, the first two players in a queue form the new team. This is a great way to get players interacting with teammates.

⚽ Add either a red or blue cone at the end of each pitch. A blue cone means one player enters for that end and a red cone means two players enter. That way the coach can ensure 1-v-1, 2-v-2 and 2-v-1 games. Observe where your players choose to go!

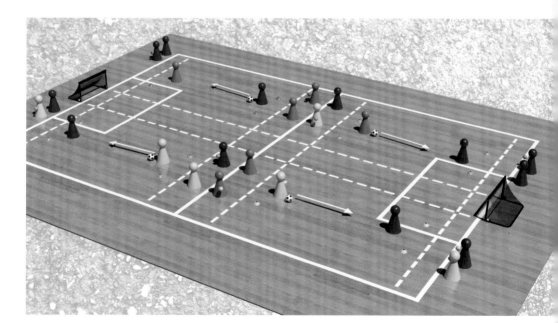

SINGLES TO DOUBLES

Setup

- Organize pitches which have two 1-v-1 channels and when combined will become a 2-v-2 pitch.

- A ball is needed for both pitches.

How It Works

1. Blues play 1-v-1 games against their red opponent.
2. Each player attacks a cone (or cones) to knock over with the ball.
3. When one player knocks over a cone, they shout out a word to signify that their 1-v-1 game is over and the game has now changed to a 2v2 (we use the word dingles which is a combination of singles and doubles, but let the players decide the magic word)!
4. The ball which knocked over the cone is now left alone; the game now becomes a 2v2 with players trying to score in the small goal with the ball from the other 1-v-1 game. Goals must be scored within the attacking half.
5. Players get five points for winning a singles match and five points for winning a doubles match. So if blue #1 knocked over the cone, with the blues beating the reds in the 2-v-2 game, blue #1 would now have 10 points.
6. Keep rotating teams and swapping players so the players keep playing against different players.

Options, Progressions and Variations

⚽ Have different versions of 1-v-1 games on different pitches (e.g. panna battle, dribble into a zone or stop ball on the line).

⚽ If you have goalkeepers, let them quickly join a pitch when they hear the magic word being shouted out and choose a goal to defend.

THREE IS THE MAGIC NUMBER

Setup

- Divide players into four teams of three players (or similar, six teams also work) with each defending a goal, as shown.

- Without letting the other teams know, each team writes down on a small whiteboard one of the following sequences:
  - 123
  - 132
  - 231
  - 213
  - 321
  - 312

How It Works

1. The coach calls out two colors which then enter the pitch to play against each other; they both attempt to score in each other's goal.

2. The first time a team is called, they send the number of players represented by the first number in their sequence. In the example shown, let's say the blues chose the sequence 321 and yellows chose the sequence 213. If the coach calls out BLUE/ YELLOW as the first game, the blues would send out three players and the yellows two players (the next time blue is called, they would send two players and the next time one).

3. Teams can decide amongst themselves which players will be the two and who will be the one but are encouraged to keep changing this.

4. Play until a goal is scored or for a set period of time.

5. When teams have played three games, they repeat their sequence.

Options, Progressions and Variations

Any team which wins against a team of three (even in a 3-v-3 game) gains a bonus point.

The coach can call out the remaining two teams while the first two teams are still playing.

Have two goalkeepers start in the middle of the pitch; they have to react quickly to defend a goal each.

THREE-SIDED 1-V-1 GAMES

Setup

- Three players play on a pitch with one ball.

- Each player defends their own small goal.

How It Works

1. The winner of the game is the player whose goal has been scored in the least number of times.
2. This rule means the players constantly change from being the defender faced with an overload to the attacker with the ball, or the supporting attacker. Also, due to this rule, two players will not be able to always gang up on the same player.
3. Players have to be alert since their goal can be attacked at any time; your players will continually try to deceive the other two players in order to score in the other goals.
4. Allow goals to be scored in both directions.
5. After every two minutes allow a rest and check how many goals have been scored in each goal.

Options, Progressions and Variations

- Play a 2-v-2-v-2 game with the same rules.

- Add more goals and players (e.g. 1v1v1 with 4 goals).

TOP TRUMPS CHAMPIONS

Setup

⚽ Each player is given one Top Trumps soccer card.

⚽ Create some suitable 1-v-1 pitches in a line next to each other.

⚽ Divide players evenly between the pitches.

⚽ A champion starts at one end of each pitch; the challengers wait at the other end.

⚽ The pitch nearest the left is called Champions League; the next, The Premiership; the next, The Championship; League 1 and League 2 complete the pitches.

How It Works

1. The champion takes on the first challenger in a 1-v-1 battle. If the champion wins, he or she stays champion and the challenger goes to the back of the line on the respective pitch.If the challenger wins, he or she becomes the champion and the previous champion goes to the back of the queue.

2. THIS IS THE TOP TRUMPS BIT! When the coach calls "STOP," the current champion gets promoted (apart from the Champions League winner) to the next pitch. B UT before going, they select a Top Trump category. The remaining players compare their cards and the player with the lowest score gets relegated to the pitch to the right (except on the League 2 pitch).

3. Players move up and down as the above, whenever the coach calls stop.

Options, Progressions and Variations

🦵 Instead of the coach calling "Stop," all the games stop if a player achieves a panna; that player shouts "PANNA!" and the players move up and down as before.

🦵 Do a 2-v-2 competition; when players move up or go down they must then get a new partner before the next round.

🦵 All players get a new card before each round.

TRIPLE CHALLENGE

Setup

- Organize an area as shown with a defender or guard (green players) in each outside area.

- A goalkeeper protects each goal.

- Attackers and dribblers (yellow players) have a ball each and wait outside the area without a goal.

How It Works

1. Each attacker has three challenges to complete and gain points:
   - Can they dribble past the first guard (who is also dribbling a ball) into the middle safe zone without getting tagged?
   - Can they then dribble into one of the three squares and beat the defender who doesn't have a ball?
   - Can they score past the goalkeeper?

2. Yellow #1 is shown completing the challenge.

Options, Progressions and Variations

- A version for those who like a bit of chaos:

  - If the attacker is tagged by the first guard, they swap places.
  - If the attacker is tackled by the second defender, who is then able to dribble into the safe zone, they swap places.
  - If the attacker doesn't score past the goalkeeper, they swap places.

🏃 Some defenders in the second square also have to dribble a ball.

🏃 Attackers work as a pair.

🏃 Have a defender and a neutral player in the middle square.

🏃 Each goal represents a different finish (e.g. left goal must be weaker foot finish; middle goal must try to go around the goalkeeper; right goal must be a curling shot).

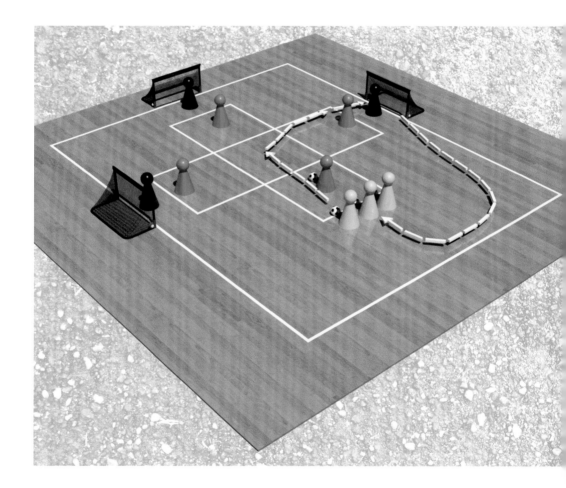

WEMBLEY CHAOS

Setup

- This is a chaotic version of the street or park game of Wembley, or World Cup, which kids have played for years!

- Organize multiple pitches for Wembley where players can score into one goal (four pitches are shown here).

- Divide players into teams and place one player from each team on each pitch.

- For those who don't know, Wembley is a 1-v-1-v-1-v-1 game where individuals battle to score goals.

- Bibs can be used but are not needed!

How It Works

1. Games start as usual with players playing against each other to try and score. In the traditional version when players score, they go through to the next round—this isn't the case here.
2. In this version, if a player scores, they move to another pitch and join in that game (shown here by the red player on the right hand pitch). You decide whether they record their goal on a whiteboard, by the side of the pitch, or whether they just have to remember how many goals they score.
3. On the new pitch, the red player can combine with their teammate. It may become a 2-v-1-v-1-v-1 game on the new pitch, leaving a 1-v-1-v-1-v-1 game on the old pitch.
4. The only exception to this rule is when there are only two players on a pitch and someone scores. On this occasion, the goal scorer still swaps pitches but is replaced by a teammate who was on the pitch they joined. Each pitch always has at least a 1-v-1 game on it. At the end of a set time period, which team scored the most goals?

Options, Progressions and Variations

⚽ Each team takes it in turn to be the goalkeepers.

⚽ Play Wembley Doubles: when a player scores they move pitches but swap with one of their players on that pitch so they have a new partner.

25 SMALL-SIDED SOCCER GAMES

Developing Problem-Solving and Decision-Making Skills in Soccer Players

GOAL CHANGERS

Players will learn how to score in a particular goal that keeps changing, making them react and adapt to changing patterns.

Setup

One team made up of three colors (red, blue and yellow) plays against another team (green). The multicolored team attacks three goals while the green team attacks one goal.

How It Works

1. The blue players can only score in the blue goal (marked with blue cones on the posts or placed behind the net as shown in the picture) and it is the same for the red and yellow players.
2. The green goalkeeper (or two keepers) has to cover all three goals.

Options, Progressions and Variations

- The coach can keep switching the cones so that the players have to keep scanning the area and adapting to the changing picture. The coach may also have some of the same colors behind the goal (e.g. if no yellow cones are behind the goals the yellow players should drop to defend).

- Colors CANNOT score in their colored goal (e.g. blues CANNOT score in the blue goal).

- Keep changing bibs so that players experience both elements of the game.

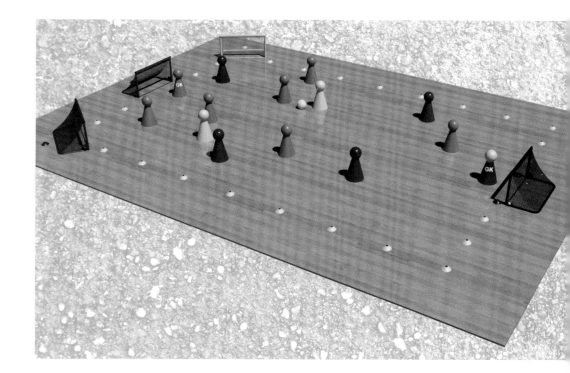

BONUS BALLS

In this game the value of the goal depends on which ball is in play...

Setup

- A normal game takes place between two evenly matched teams.

- Five balls are placed at the side of the pitch. Before the game starts, the players decide which ball is worth five points, which ball is worth four points, and so on.

- It helps if five different balls are used (e.g. different sized balls or different coloured balls). If five different balls are not available, place five of the same balls on different colored cones.

How It Works

1. The coach plays in one of the balls to start the game.
2. If a goal is scored that goal is worth the value of that ball (e.g. if the ball worth five points is used, the team earns five points).
3. If a ball goes off the pitch (e.g. throw-in) or play is stopped (e.g. free kick) the coach has the option of playing in a different ball to continue play so the value of the next goal constantly changes. This way the coach can keep the game close and exciting (e.g. when a team that is losing has a corner or penalty, the coach might change the ball to a higher scoring ball).
4. Can players adapt to the different types of balls used?
5. Do teams adapt their tactics depending on the score and the value of the ball currently in play?
6. The coach can control the level of chaos by how rapidly they change the balls being used.

Options, Progressions and Variations

🦵 Choose a trigger which allows the team to opt whether they want a ball change or not (e.g. if they save a shot on target, if they have a goal kick).

🦵 The player that puts the ball out for a throw-in has to quickly retrieve the ball and put it back on the empty cone while the coach immediately plays in another ball to the team that would have had the throw-in.

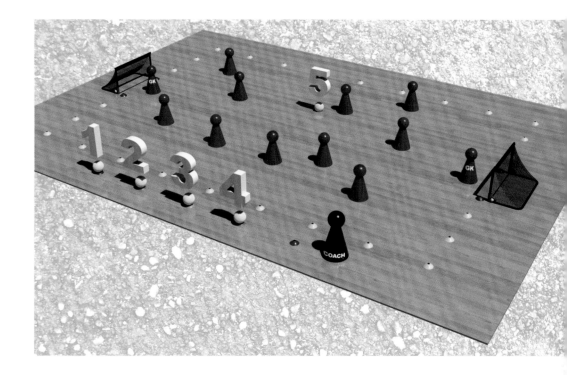

3-2-1

Everyone must touch the ball before a goal can be scored or everyone must score.

Setup

Set up a normal small-sided game.

How It Works

1. Each player starts with a value of three points. When they score their first goal of the game, it counts as three points for their team.
2. Once a player scores their value lowers to two points and the next goal they score is worth two points.
3. Their next goal, and any additional goals, is worth one point.
4. Every so often allow the players to have a time out to adjust their positions based on the players' values.

Options, Progressions and Variations

The value of the goal is made up of the value of the player who scored and the player that passed it to them. In the diagram the red team's goal would be worth six points, and the blue team's goal would be worth four points.

PLAYER ANALYSIS

This game helps players to recognize and analyze patterns in the game and adjust their tactics accordingly.

Setup

Two teams play a game and the coach (or other players) observe certain aspects of one or both teams.

How It Works

1. Different aspects of the game are recorded using cones on the side of the pitch. Each aspect has a different color cone (e.g. shots are marked by orange cones, passes by yellow, dribbles by green). Successful aspects, such as shots on target, are marked by a cone placed the usual way; unsuccessful aspects, such as a shot off target, are marked by an upside-down cone. For example a dribble in which the ball was lost would be marked by an upside-down green cone.

2. After a set period of time, ask the players to analyze the cones, interpret what they think it means and suggest ways to improve aspects of the game.

Options, Progressions and Variations

- Allow the players to decide what aspects they would like to have analyzed.

- In a match? Consider whether this would be a good exercise for players to do when being a substitute and whether it could help players evaluate their tactics at half time.

PANNA PUT-BACK

In this game players have the options of scoring goals or regaining balls.

Setup

Each team defends and attacks a line of balls on cones.

How It Works

1. Teams attack their opponent's targets trying to knock over the balls.
2. Players can regain and replace one of their team's own targets by making a panna (nutmeg).
3. Which team has the most targets at the end of a set period of time?

Options, Progressions and Variations

- Let the players decide what allows them to replace a ball (e.g. a no-touch turn, tackling an opponent, passing the ball).

- Play with four teams each defending their own line but attacking the other three lines. Teams can combine to attack. The team with the most targets left wins.

- Allow play to happen behind the targets (as in ice hockey).

1-V-1 CHANNEL

In this game two normal small-sided games take place but with extra goals up for grabs for players who are successful in the 1-v-1 channel.

Setup

- Set up two pitches with a 1-v-1 channel between them. Additional channels at the side of the pitch are optional.

- One defender from each team is placed in the middle of the channel.

- A spare ball is placed on a cone in the middle of each pitch.

How It Works

1. Goals can be scored in the usual way (as shown by the yellow team in the top pitch in the diagram).

2. However, at any time during the game, a player can dribble into the channel and take on the waiting opposition defender in the channel. The challenging player must dribble to the end line to score a goal. In the diagram, yellow #1 from the bottom pitch has dribbled into the middle channel to take on the waiting blue defender.

3. When this happens, the remaining players on the pitch quickly take the ball from the cone and carry on the game; the team without the player in the channel will have a temporary overload. In the bottom pitch shown, blue #1 reacts first and takes possession of the new ball.

4. When the 1-v-1 game is over (i.e. either the attacker is successful, the defender has possession of the ball, or the ball has gone out of the channel), the attacker runs the ball back to the cone and rejoins the game. Players can only enter a channel when the teams are even on their pitch.

5. If a player from one pitch has entered the middle channel, a player from the same team on the other pitch cannot enter it as well, but can enter the side channel if being used.

6. Which team can score the most goals in a set period of time?

Options, Progressions and Variations

⟿ If players are not entering the 1-v-1 channel, increase the points for a successful 1-v-1 challenge.

⟿ When an attacker's 1-v-1 game is over, they stay in the channel, become the defender and are replaced in the game by the existing channel defender from their team.

⟿ Allow players from the same team playing on different pitches to both enter the middle channel. The defender will have two 1-v-1 games to deal with when this happens.

⟿ Have different 1-v-1 challenges in the channels (e.g. panna competition, head tennis).

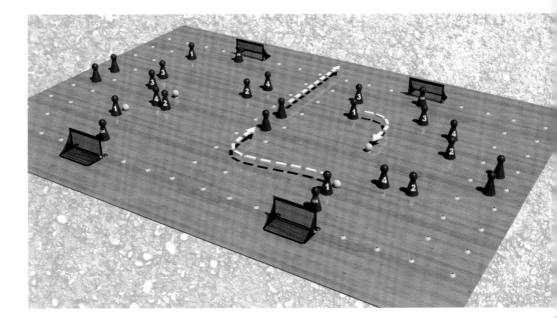

STEAL A BALL, LOSE A PLAYER

In this game, teams are rewarded for scoring a goal by stealing the match ball, but they lose a player to the other team. Which team can steal five match balls first?

Setup

- Start with an evenly matched game.

- Each team has equal amount of empty cones by the side of the pitch.

How It Works

1. The game starts as normal until the first goal is scored.
2. The team that scores the first goal gets to keep the ball and place it on one of their cones.
3. However, they now lose a player to the opposition team (the other team or coach select the player to join their team). In an 8-v-8 game, the game would now restart as a 9-v-7 game.
4. To help inclusion, players can only be transferred once, or a maximum of two times. If using goalkeepers, it is best if they cannot be transferred.
5. This process repeats every time a goal is scored. The team that scores a goal gets a ball but loses a player. In the diagram you can see that the game is currently 10v6 as the reds have had two players taken by the yellows and are winning 4-2.
6. Which team can steal five balls and fill their cones first?
7. The players on the team when the fifth cone is filled are the winners and gain the points.
8. Choose new teams and play again!

Options, Progressions and Variations

⚽ The winning team gains the number of points related to the number of spare cones held by their opposition at the end of the game (i.e. if the red team in the diagram score the next goal they would all gain 3 points because the yellow team has three empty cones).

⚽ Use a variety of balls for each round (e.g. size 3, tennis ball, futsal).

⚽ The players transferred can be selected at random (e.g. the coach pulls a name out of a hat, players swap in order of their birthday).

⚽ Play this as a 2-v-2 game with each team having two cones to fill.

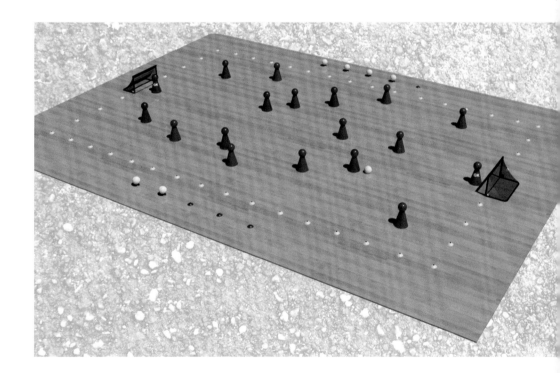

SET PIECE CHALLENGE

In this game players take ownership and design creative set pieces and dead ball situations (e.g. free kicks).

Setup

Organize four groups who will create and practice set pieces.

How It Works

1. Stage 1: Planning
   - Players design, practice and refine a set piece or dead ball situation (e.g. attacking indirect free kick). The players might be given examples and ideas to help BUT cannot simply copy the idea.

2. Stage 2: Game
   - A normal game takes place where, as a result of stage 1, each team will have two planned set pieces.
   - These free kicks will be used if a free kick is awarded BUT also if a pre-determined situation occurs (e.g. a shot on target that the goalkeeper parries or deflects).
   - In this example, if the red team have a shot tipped around the post by the blue goalkeeper, the red team is awarded an attacking indirect free kick. The blue team defends the free kick as they would in a game.
   - Group A gets to go first and tries their free kick. The next time this situation happens group B will try their free kick.

3. Allow opportunities for the players to reflect on their free kicks and go back to stage 1 to have an opportunity to improve and refine their set pieces.

Options, Progressions and Variations

⚡ Goals resulting from free kicks are worth more.

⚡ Group A are in charge of one type of set piece (e.g. indirect free kicks in the penalty area) and group B are in charge of another (e.g. corners).

⚡ Group A and group B have to teach each other their free kicks so that during the game any four players take responsibility for the decision and execution of the free kick.

⚡ Allow the players to decide which ones they would like to use in their next match.

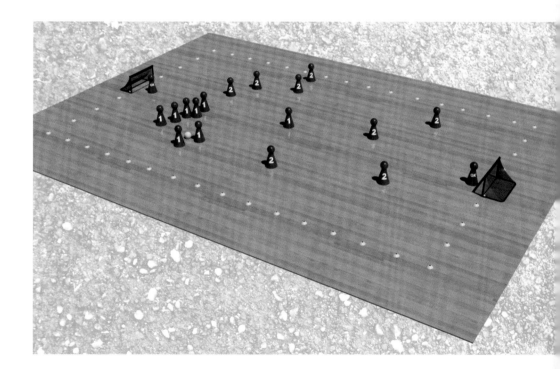

FOUR-GOAL CARNAGE

In this game teams continually play against different teams, on different pitch shapes, in high-tempo games.

Setup

Organize a pitch as shown in the diagram with four goals and a neutral square in the middle of the pitch. One ball is placed in the square and the coach controls the other balls.

How It Works

1. All four teams start in their area of the pitch, as shown in the diagram.
2. The coach calls out a color and that team runs into the square, collects the ball and then moves into one of the other three areas (in the diagram they choose to play yellow). This triggers a game between blue and yellow. The game takes place only in the blue and yellow areas of the pitch. The middle square is in play but is a no-tackle zone. If the blue team had chosen to go straight across and play the green team, the pitch would have been a kind of hour-glass shape. If the ball goes off the pitch, the game is restarted as normal.
3. As soon as one game is underway, the coach plays a ball onto the other pitch for the remaining two teams to play.
4. Both games finish when ONE TEAM scores and that team steals the point (i.e. only one team can get a point each time).
5. When a goal is scored, the teams and balls are reset and the coach calls out a color again.
6. Which team has scored the most goals after a set period of time?

Options, Progressions and Variations

⚽ Allow tackles in the square.

⚽ Allow the teams to play anywhere on the pitch, but they can still only score in one goal.

⚽ Award a point for the team that scores, but also subtract a point for the team that concedes.

RANDOM COLOR OVERLOAD

In this game teams will constantly experience different games of varying numbers.

Setup

- Split the group into two teams (2x6 works well)

- The coach has six different colored cones and a set of balls on the half way line.

- Each team assign a number 1-6 to each color - the teams tell the coach but not the other team.

- So for example the blue team may have something like:

  - White = 1
  - Blue = 2
  - Green = 3
  - Yellow = 4
  - Orange = 5
  - Red = 6

- The other team will most likely assigned different numbers to the colors.

- The coach may want to record the choices!

How It Works

1. The coach begins the game by picking up a colored cone. In the example shown, the coach has picked up the green cone. The blue team had assigned the number 3 to this so they send out three players. The red team had assigned the number 1 so only one player comes out. The two teams will play a 3-v-1 game.

2. The coach plays the ball to the team with the overload. If the game is equally matched, the coach passes to the team currently losing.
3. The game continues until a goal is scored, for a set period of time, or until the ball has left the pitch a set number of times.
4. After this, another cone is selected and another randomly sized game begins.
5. Which team has scored the most goals after a set number of matches?
6. Encourage the players to ensure that everyone on their team gets equal playing time.

Options, Progressions and Variations

🏃 Get one team to select their numbers first, then tell the opposition team these choices before the opposition choose their numbers.

🏃 Hold up another cone while the game is in place. The teams have to quickly adjust their team and react to the new color and numbers.

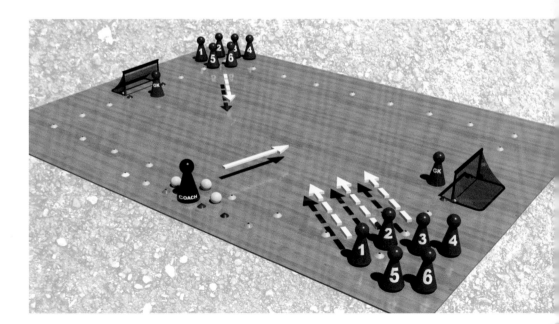

LIFE IN A BOTTLE (OUTSIDE TRAINING SESSION ONLY)

In this game teams will continually play against different teams, on different pitch shapes, in high-tempo games.

Setup

- Four teams each defend a bottle filled with water placed inside a line.

- One ball is used.

How It Works

1. The winning team in this game are the team with the most amount of water left in their bottle at the end of the game.
2. Teams try to knock over the opposition's bottles with the ball in order to spill as much water as possible!
3. Teams can combine so at times it could be three teams against one team but of course teams could turn or change at any time!

Options, Progressions and Variations

- Allow teams to put their bottle anywhere on the pitch except the corners.

- If a player makes a panna (nutmeg), they get a free shot at that player's bottle.

- Use two balls.

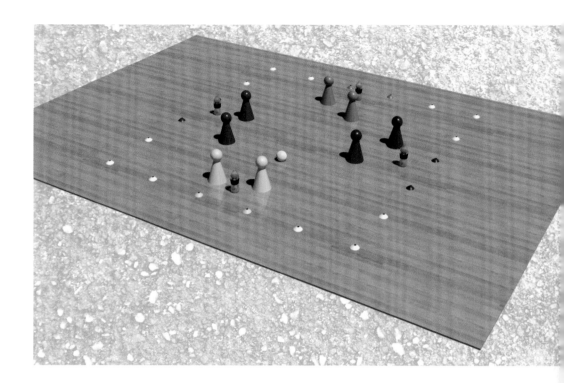

BANK IT

In this game teams decide whether to bank their goals or continue to accumulate points (like in the game show The Weakest Link!).

Setup

Just organize two teams ready to play!

How It Works

1. Two teams play a normal game until the first goal is scored. As in a normal game this goal is worth one point. The team which scored can decide to bank this goal and keep the point or decide to accumulate points.
2. If they bank the goal, then the next goal they score is also worth one point, and they must decide again whether to bank the goal or try to accumulate points.
3. If they decide to accumulate and are able to score the next goal, it is worth 3 points, and they must decide again whether to bank or accumulate. Banked points cannot be taken away.
4. If a team takes the risk to accumulate points and fails to score the next goal, then they lose the points already built up but not those previously banked.
5. Accumulation points:
    - 1 goal = 1 point
    - 2 consecutive goals = 3 points
    - 3 consecutive goals = 6 points
    - 4 consecutive goals = 10 points
    - 5 consecutive goals = 15 points

Options, Progressions and Variations

When a team decides to accumulate points, they also gain a condition to which they must adhere (e.g. first time finish only, must play out of own half for a set time period). This is a good way for teams achieving success to be challenged further.

BLOCKADE

In this game players need to look up before shooting or they may find that their goal is blocked.

Setup

- This game is shown played as four 1-v-1 games but can quickly progress to two 2-v-2 games or one 4-v-4 game.

- Both teams attack 4 small goals.

- The games are continuous and play for a set period of time.

How It Works

1. Players or teams can score in any of the four goals they are attacking but in addition to having to get past the other team, they also have to get past a blocker and a goalkeeper who defends all four goals.

2. The blocker is a defender who works behind the goals to try and deny a goal-scoring opportunity by carrying a cone and placing it behind a goal. This goal cannot be scored in now.

3. The blocker assesses the position of the players and the goalkeeper, and decides which goal needs covering.

4. The players on the pitch need to see which goal is blocked, see the goalkeeper's position, and attack accordingly.

Options, Progressions and Variations

In a 2-v-2 or 4-v-4 game, play with two blockers behind each goal. They work together as a defensive pair working together to cover the goals.

In a 2-v-2 or 4-v-4 game, play with two blockers who share a cone. One of the blockers can enter the pitch to defend but must leave and swap with the other blocker every 20 seconds.

If you don't have small goals with nets, the blockers can run and stand behind the goal to stop the ball from traveling past a line behind them.

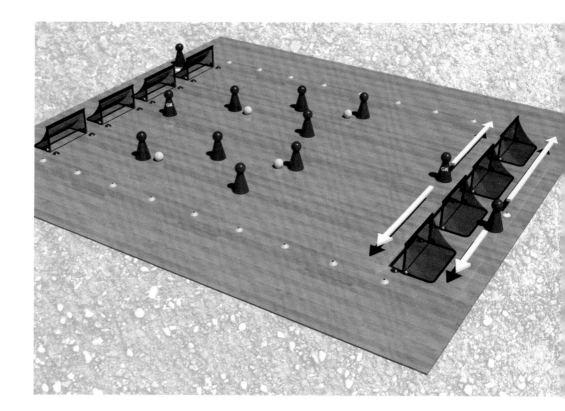

HANDS AND FEET

In this game you need the skills of an outfield player and the skills of a goalkeeper!

Setup

Play a small-sided game on a normal pitch setup.

How It Works

1. The rules are very simple. When a team has possession of the ball, they are outfield players in that they cannot use their hands.
2. However, when a team is not in possession of the ball, they are all goalkeepers anywhere on the pitch!
3. For example, the players not in possession can catch, dive, deflect to intercept a pass, cross or shot and can tackle as a goalkeeper would in a 1-v-1 situation.
4. If the goalkeeping team regains possession, they have to quickly become outfield players and drop the ball to the floor for themselves or distribute it to a teammate to control as an outfield player.

Options, Progressions and Variations

↝ If players drop a cross or aerial pass, then the other team regains possession.

↝ Goalkeepers must distribute the ball to a teammate after gaining the ball.

↝ Only some players are subject to the goalkeeper rule so attackers adapt to which player is coming to tackle them.

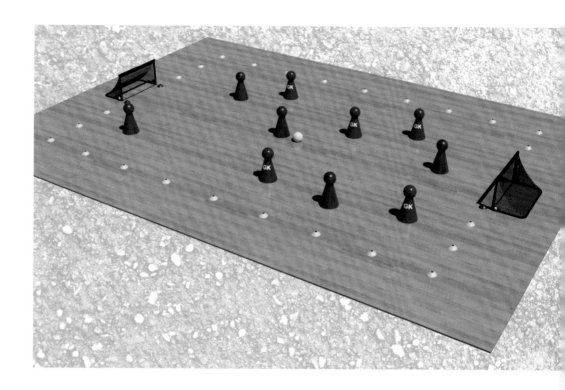

WAYS TO SCORE A GOAL

In this game two teams play a normal game but are provided with a set of ways that they can score a goal for bonus points.

Setup

🏃 Design a list of ten ways to score a goal.

🏃 Two teams play on a normal small-sided pitch.

How It Works

1. Two teams select three ways to score a goal from the list of ten. If they score in this way it is worth three points. Any other goal is still worth one point.

2. Examples of ways to score a goal:

   🏃 A goal that results from the ball being played through the three thirds (shown here by the green team)

   🏃 A goal that is set back from the attacking third into the middle third for a shot (shown here by the blue team)

   🏃 From a corner (shown by yellow team)

   🏃 A goal from a combination of three one-touch passes (shown here by red team)

3. Be creative in the ways used to score bonus points (use examples of goals scored on the TV).

Options, Progressions and Variations

- First team to complete the full house wins.

- Goals can only be scored in the described way.

- Only one team has the list.

- Teams don't know the list and have to work out the ways they can score by being told "Yes" or "No" by the coach after a goal has been scored.

- Allow the players to create the list.

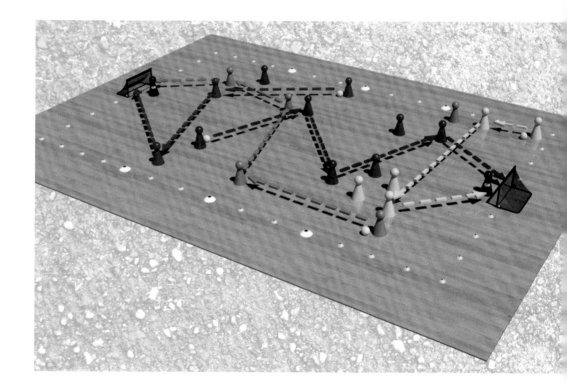

SHOOTING COCONUT SHY

In this game shooting accuracy is really important!

Setup

Set up a pitch for a small-sided game but with two or three cones with balls on them in each goal mouth.

How It Works

1. If a team scores without knocking a ball off a cone then they get a goal BUT also have to add another cone/ball in their opponent's goalmouth. This makes it more difficult for the team to score again.
2. In the diagram, the red team has scored more goals as they have to negotiate six obstacles compared to the blue team who have to negotiate only four obstacles.

Options, Progressions and Variations

- Have a hotshot player on each team. If they score a goal, it is worth two points but if they knock the ball off the cone, it is a goal to the other team.

- Set a limit of balls and cones and when these are all on the pitch, the next goal wins the game.

- Allow the players to decide where the cones and balls are placed.

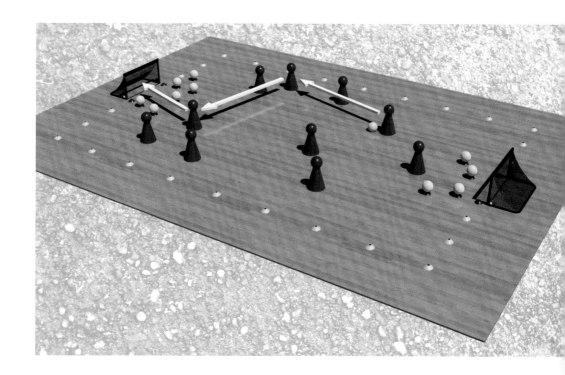

ANALYZING OPPONENTS

This game encourages players to analyze their opponent's weaknesses during a game and to devise strategies to exploit them.

Setup

Play a normal game but some players from one team (red team) have a weakness given to them which they must stick to during the game.

How It Works

1. For example:
   - The player holding the orange cone (or wearing an orange bib) only plays forward passes (or never plays forward passes).
   - The player holding the green cone (or wearing a green bib) is one footed and doesn't use their weaker foot.
   - The player holding the yellow cone (or wearing a yellow bib) never passes and looks to dribble or shoot at every opportunity.

2. The blue team players must work out how to try and make sure that the weaknesses of the other team remain weaknesses and are exploited.

Options, Progressions and Variations

- Progression 1: Allow the players to keep swapping cones to make it harder for the defenders.

- Progression 2: Some players are given the same weaknesses as before but not the cones. Can the blue players still work them out and be successful in their tactics?

 Progression 3: This time the red players are given weaknesses but the blue players are not told what they are. Can the blue players work them out and can they adapt?

 Progression 4: Tell the blue team that the red players have been given weaknesses (as in progression 3), but actually tell the red players that they have no weaknesses. Watch as the blue players still analyze the red players, replicating a process they should undergo in a match situation. This actually provides great feedback for the red players from the blue players at the end of the game.

CONE BONUS

In this game the losing team gets a little helping hand.

Setup

- Two teams play a normal small-sided game.

- At the side of the pitch are a series of cones, each with a different bonus written on them.

How It Works

1. The game begins as normal until one team (e.g. the blues) scores a goal and goes 1-0 ahead.

2. At this point (before the game is restarted), the red team picks a cone and gains the bonus written on it. Example bonuses may include:
   - The opposition can only score with their weaker foot.
   - Take one player from the opposition to play for you.
   - All your set pieces (e.g. throw-ins, goal kicks) are now corner kicks.
   - The opposition can only score from outside the area.
   - You have one player that cannot be tackled in the defending half.
   - The opposition goalkeeper comes to play for you so you have two keepers.

3. This bonus cone is placed behind the team's goal and lasts until the next goal in the game is scored. If the red team take advantage of their bonus and equalize (1-1), the cone is returned and the normal game continues. However, if the blue team score to make it 2-0, another bonus cone is selected by the red team, placed behind the goal and now both bonuses are in play. If the team with a bonus scores a goal, a bonus cone is returned. If the game is tied, no bonuses are in place. However, if three cones are behind a goal then the coach knows that team is three goals behind.

4. In essence this game continues to provide challenges for both teams without the coach interfering! Allow a timeout after the bonus is chosen so that both teams can devise their response.

Options, Progressions and Variations

🏃 Use colored cones to differentiate the bonuses, so that the least helpful bonuses are on green cones, quite helpful ones are on the yellow cones and the really helpful ones are on the red ones. Teams pick a bonus from a green cone when they first need one, then from a yellow one, then a red one.

🏃 Turn the cones over to hide the bonuses, so that the choice of bonus is random.

🏃 Allow the team that is leading to select the bonus for the losing team.

🏃 Allow players to come up with the bonuses.

🏃 Tip: If you don't want to write on your cones, just use sticky labels or write on clothespins and clip these to the cones.

IN THE ZONE

This game enables players to experience and explore different playing styles while giving them ownership over the tactics used.

Setup

Divide the pitches into zones; here three horizontal zones are used but you can have as many as you like and different sizes and positions.

How It Works

1. Teams are presented with a menu of conditions (a list of ten works well), for example;

    - Can only play forward

    - Must attempt to dribble when receiving the ball

    - Must play three passes before leaving the zone

    - Three players must combine

    - Must shoot if having a second touch

2. Teams select three conditions from the menu and assign one condition to each zone (e.g. they might assign the three-players-must-combine condition to the middle zone).

3. Each team sticks to their three rules while playing against the other team.

Options, Progressions and Variations

🏃 The other team know their opponents' rules.

🏃 Allow timeouts (evaluation time) and rules to be changed.

🏃 Allow players to come up with their own conditions based on how their favorite team plays.

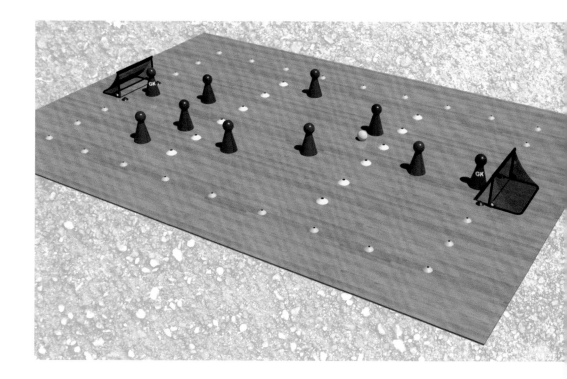

SCENARIO CARDS

In this game players are given real-life soccer scenarios and have to plan their team's tactics and strategies.

Setup

Prepare scenarios for the players to discuss and devise solutions from.

How It Works

1. Team A and team B are given the scenarios and, as teams, have to plan their tactics and strategy to reflect the scenario.
2. The game is a set time period.
3. After each goal (which may change the scenario), they have a set time period to evaluate and adapt their plan.
4. Sample scenarios:

   - It is the second leg of the Champions League semifinal. Team B is playing at home. The result from the first leg was team A 1 to team B 0. If after two legs the teams are drawn, then the team that scored the most away goals will go through to the final.
   - Team A always plays with a midfield triangle (sometimes with two holding players, sometimes with one) while team B likes to change their formation based on their opposition's formation.

5. See how your players discuss, plan, apply and adapt their tactics and strategies.

Options, Progressions and Variations

- Include some tips to encourage only positive tactics (e.g. Time-wasting is not allowed as a tactic, allow players to play in different positions so they can learn more about different aspects of the game).

- Allow players to come up with their own scenarios.

- Use real scenarios from previous games (their own games and those on TV).

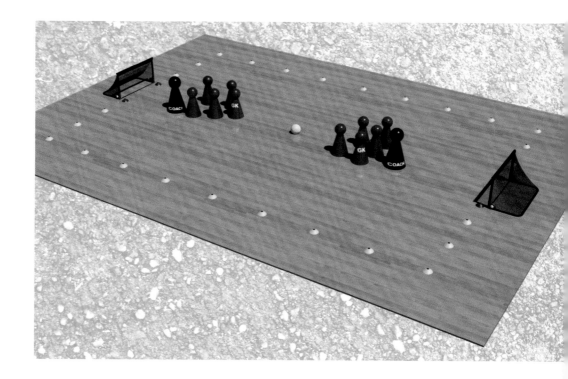

1-V-1 BONUS

In this game two matches are played as normal, but when a goal is scored the team have a chance to gain a bonus goal!

Setup

🦵 Organize two matches or pitches with a smaller 1-v-1 area between them.

🦵 Balls are placed behind each goal and teams know which goal (or line) they will attack on the 1-v-1 pitch.

How It Works

1. The two games are played as normal. The winners will be the team that scores the most goals.

2. When a goal is scored, the player that scored the goal quickly runs and collects a ball from their goal on the 1-v-1 pitch. An opposition player from THE OTHER PITCH must quickly run onto the 1-v-1 pitch to stop them scoring or to regain the ball and score themselves. The other opposition players are allowed to alert players from the other pitch that an attack is about to take place.

3. Any goal scored on the 1-v-1 pitch counts as another goal. So a player who scores in the main game can gain an additional goal by scoring on the 1-v-1 pitch.

4. The main games continue while the 1-v-1 games takes place, so there will be overloads on the main pitches while this happens.

5. If another goal is scored on the main pitches while the 1-v-1 game is taking place, the goal scorer and opposition player are still allowed to join the 1-v-1 pitch, so there may be more than one 1-v-1 game taking place!

6. At the end, add up all the goals and see which team is victorious!

Options, Progressions and Variations

Pair players up so that if blue #1 scored on one pitch it is red #1 on the other pitch that must come and defend.

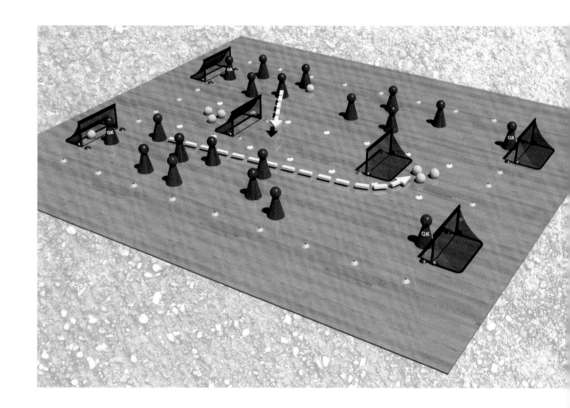

5-4-3-2-1-0 COUNTDOWN

Try this game to get your players reacting to and exploring different styles of play (e.g. patient build-up versus quick counterattack).

Setup

Use a pitch suitable for a small-sided game.

How It Works

1. The winning team will be the first to score six goals, but these goals must be scored in the following ways:
   - After five passes
   - After four passes
   - After three passes
   - After two passes
   - After one pass
   - After zero passes (i.e. player regains possession and scores themselves)

2. Goals can be scored in any order.

3. When one of the above list has been scored that team cannot score in that way again (if they do it does not count).

4. Which team scores the six goals first?

Options, Progressions and Variations

Divide the list of ways goals must be scored between both teams (e.g. one team must score with zero, one and two passes while the other team must score with three, four and five passes). Play first to three goals.

Make one team count down from five to zero passes and the other team count up from zero to five passes.

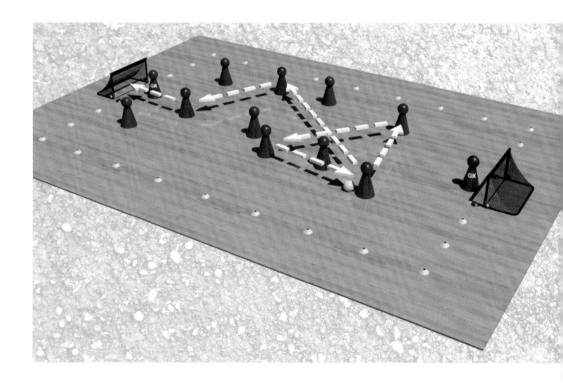

CONSECUTIVE GOALS

Two teams play a series of matches where the tactics and decision making increase with each match.

Setup

Just a pitch and two teams!

How It Works

1. GAME 1: The first game ends when the first goal is scored.

2. GAME 2: In the second game, the team that won the first game must score two consecutive goals to win, while the team that lost the first game still only needs one goal to win the match.

3. GAMES 3+: This sequence continues in that when a team is successful in their challenge (e.g. score two consecutive goals), their challenge is upped in the next game (e.g. score three consecutive goals).

4. For example, team A must score three consecutive goals to win and team B must score two consecutive goals to win. Tactics will therefore change depending on the current score! Allow timeouts when relevant. The game may take a while to finish!

5. Decide the finishing point; for example if a team wins by scoring three consecutive goals, they win, the teams are reselected and the challenge begins again.

Options, Progressions and Variations

- Make the challenge harder; after a goal is scored, the goal is made smaller so not only does the team need consecutive goals but each consecutive goal is harder to score.

- The player who scored the last goal is not allowed to score the next goal.

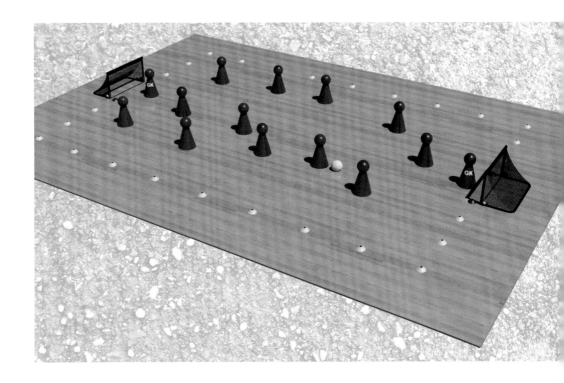

CHOOSE YOUR GOAL

In this game players can choose the goal they shoot in depending on the position they shoot from.

Setup

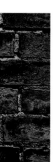

- The pitch is divided into three different colored thirds. A smaller pitch in which goals can realistically be scored from anywhere works best.

- Using the same colors, each team has a big goal to score in, a medium-sized goal to score in and a small goal to score in.

- The color of the small goal is the same color as the closest third, the middle goal matches the color of the middle third, and the big goal matches the color of the furthest third.

How It Works

1. Two teams play against each other in a normal game with one ball.
2. However, a goal scored from within the closest third must be scored in the smallest goal (shown by the red team). Likewise a goal from the middle third must go through the middle set of goals (green goal), and a long-range shot from the furthest third must go through the big goal (shown by the blue team).

Options, Progressions and Variations

- Award different points for long-range goals or first-time finishes.

- Play on a short and wide pitch for more goal-scoring opportunities.

➤ Restrict players to one or two zones. They must swap zones with another player if they score.

➤ Instead of zones have colored squares marked out on the pitch which correspond to different colored goals.

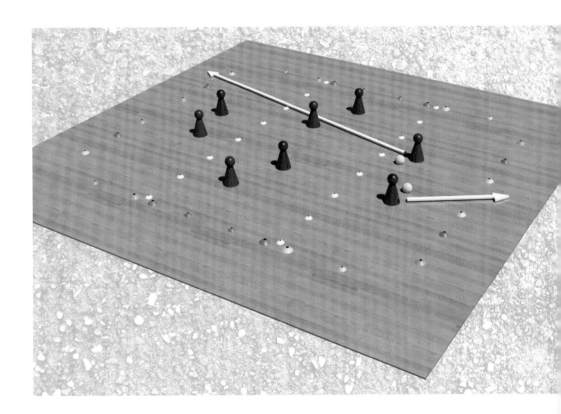

REMOVE THE BIBS

In this game players will have the choice and ownership of the order of their individual challenges and two team challenges.

Setup

🏃 Two teams play a normal timed game.

🏃 Team A is the non-bibs and they have free play (shown by the blues).

🏃 Each player on team B wears three bibs of different colors (e.g. blue, yellow and red).

🏃 The players choose the order in which they wear the bibs and each player can have a different combination (e.g. blue on first, then red, then yellow on top).

How It Works

1. Team Challenge 1 (Teams A and B): Both teams try to win the game as normal.

2. Team Challenge 2 (for team B): In the set time period the team tries to remove as many bibs as possible. This is how they do it:

   🏃 The players with the red bibs on the top remove this bib when they tackle an opponent and keep possession. (Another colored bib will now show.)

   🏃 The players with the blue bibs on top remove this bib when they dribble past an opponent, panna an opponent or pull off an outrageous piece of skill! (Another colored bib will now show).

   🏃 The players with the yellow bibs on the top remove this bib when they score a goal or provide an assist for a goal. (Another colored bib will now show.)

   🏃 When a player reveals a new bib, that player has a new challenge to complete before removing the next bib.

3. Which team won the game?

4. How many bibs did team B remove?

5. Was a player able to remove all three of their bibs?

6. After a set time the teams swap over and team A will wear the bibs.

Options, Progressions and Variations

Only give the players two bibs each.

Allow the players to decide what challenges the bibs represent.

Yellow bibs are individual personal challenges decided by the coach.

For maximum chaos, have both teams wearing bibs!

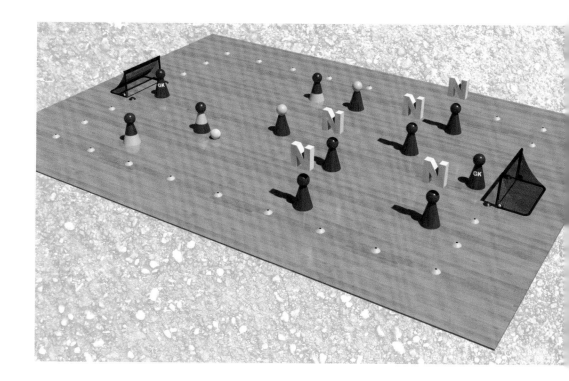

SUMMARY

This book has charted the basic concepts that underpin street soccer. It has shown that, far from being a frivolous activity for enjoyment only, play is in fact one of the most important tools available to the coach. This book is the epitome of practical application particularly given the conceptual foundation of soccer as a sport. The book has also given the coach an insight into how the sports brain works or operates. In this way it anticipates that the concepts that we have discussed in this book will make the learning process enjoyable for everyone. Welcome to the exciting world that is street soccer!

BIBLIOGRAPHY

All LYBIO. (1987, June 24th). *Leo Messi – This Is My Formula.* Retrieved from Adidas My Formula: http://lybio.net/adidas-my-formula-leo-messi-this-is-my-formula/sports/

Axel Springer. (2015). *Principles of Leadership.* Retrieved from AG: https://www.axelspringer.de/en/artikel/Principles-of-Leadership-at-Axel-Springer-AG_40849.html

Chaves, E. (2013, November 9th). *Play and Learning: One Brazilian's View.* Retrieved from LEGO University: https://unilego.wordpress.com/2013/11/09/play_and_learning_one_brazilians_view/

Colvin, G. (2008, October 21st). *Why Talent Is Overrated: The Conventional Wisdom about „Natural" Talent Is a Myth. The Real Path to Great Performance Is a Matter of Choice.* Retrieved from Fortune Magazine: http://archive.fortune.com/2008/10/21/magazines/fortune/talent_colvin.fortune/index.htm

Crisfield, P., Cabral, P., & Carpenter, F. (2003). *The Successful Coach Guidelines for Coaching Practice.* Leeds: The National Coaching Foundation.

Davis, P. H. (2004). *Beatitudes of Learning: Eight Principles for Optimizing all Learning Situations.* Bloomington (IND): Author House.

Gordon, S. (2013, October 4th). *There is no Left-Brain & Right-Brain Thinking.* Retrieved from Special Ed Post: http://specialedpost.org/2013/10/04/there-is-no-left-brain-right-brain-thinking/

Itsagoal. (2013, August). *Football Coaching hClub Volunteers to Encourage Enthusiasm, Flair and Creative Innovation in Young Footballers.* Retrieved from Football Coaching: http://www.itsagoal.net/itsa-goal-posts/football-coaching/

Loewenstein, G. (1994). The Psychology of Curiosity: A Review and Reinterpretation. *Psychological Bulletin, 116* (1), 75-98.

Maclean, P. D. (1987). Triune Brain. In G. Adelman, *Encyclopedia of Neuroscience* (pp. 1235-1237). Cambridge (MA): Birkhauser Boston.

Marshall, N. (2014). *The Teacher's Introduction to Attachment: Practical Essentials for Teachers, Carers and School Support Staff.* London: Jessica Kingsley Publishers.

McIntyre, M. C. (2004). A Comparison of the Physiological Profiles of Elite Gaelic Footballers, Hurlers, and Soccer Players. *British Journal of Sports Medicine, 39* (1), 437-439.

Micciche, D. (2015). *Training with MK Dons U12/13's.* Retrieved from Soccer Coaching International Web Special: http://www.soccercoachinginternational.com/pdf/Dan%20Micciche-MK%20Dons.pdf

Mitra, S. (2013, February). *Build a School in the Cloud.* Retrieved from TED Talk: https://www.ted.com/talks/sugata_mitra_build_a_school_in_the_cloud?language=en

Northern Tigers. (2015). *Coaching Philosophy.* Retrieved from NSFA: http://northerntigersfc.com.au/website/default.asp?page=coachingphilosophy2

Ostwald-Kowald, T. (2013, January 18th). *Understanding Your Student's Learning Style: The Theory of Multiple Intelligences.* Retrieved from Connections Academy: http://www.connectionsacademy.com/blog/posts/2013-01-18/Understanding-Your-Student-s-Learning-Style-The-Theory-of-Multiple-Intelligences.aspx

STREET SOCCER

Paul, R., & Elder, L. (2006). The Art of Socratic Questioning. *Critical Thinking Concepts and Tools.* Tomales, California, USA: The Foundation for Critical Thinking.

Peter, L. J. (1979). *Peter's Quotations: Ideas for Our Time* (2nd ed.). New York: Bantam Books.

Pychyl, T. A. (2008, May 10th). *Motivation, Procrastination, and Yeats.* Retrieved from Psychology Today Blog: https://www.psychologytoday.com/blog/dont-delay/200805/education-is-not-the-filling-pail-the-lighting-fire

Ramsden, K. (2015, September 2nd). *No One Knows.* Retrieved from Adventures in Life, Brainwaves on Business: http://kelseyramsden.com/no-one-knows/

Rata, N. (2011, February 20th). *Copy of Communities of Practice at Unitec.* Retrieved from Discussion of the evolution of Communities of Practice supporting: https://prezi.com/itwpbtuhojni/copy-of-communities-of-practice-at-unitec/

Rother, M. (2011, December). *The Five Coaching Kata Questions.* Retrieved from Slideshare: http://www.slideshare.net/mike734/the-five-questions

Ryan, R. M., & Deci, E. L. (2000). Intrinsic and Extrinsic Motivations: Classic Definitions and New Directions. *Contemporary Educational Psychology, 25* (1), 54-67.

The International Street Soccer Association. (2015). *Street Soccer Training Creativity.* Retrieved from ISSA Soccer: http://www.issasoccer.com/issa-street-soccer-training-creativity/

Turnell, M. (2013, October 10th). *Intrinsic vs Extrinsic Motivation.* Retrieved from Motivation and Engagement: https://m0tlv8me.wordpress.com/2013/10/10/intrinsic-vs-extrinsic-motivation/

US Play Coalition. (2011, July). *Newsletter.* Retrieved from Clemson University Resources: http://usplaycoalition.clemson.edu/resources/newsletter/2011july.pdf

Vallerand, R. J. (2008). On the Psychology of Passion: In Search of What Makes People's Lives Most Worth Living. *Canadian Psychology, 49* (1), 1-13.

Vallerand, R. J., Salvy, S. J., Mageau, G. A., Elliot, A. J., Denis, P., Grouzet, F. M., & Blanchard, C. (2007). On the Role of Passion in Performance. *Journal of Personality, 75* (1), 505-534.

Young, D. (2011). *Great Funny Quotes: Sweeten your Life with Laughter.* Round Rock (TX): Wind Runner Press.

Young, G. (2012, May 15th). *What are the Ingredients to Make an Elite Soccer Player?* Retrieved from Monday Morning Centreback: https://mondaymorningcentreback. wordpress.com/2012/05/15/what-are-the-ingredients-to-make-an-elite-soccer-player/

CREDITS

Cover and Jacket design:	Sannah Inderelst
Cover photo:	©Thinkstock/iStock
	©picture-alliance/dpa
Layout and Typesetting:	Sannah Inderelst
Photos inside:	Darren Laver
	©Thinkstock/iStock
Graphics:	Jonathan Brammer
Editing:	Jillian Evans, Kristina Tegtmeier